IATEFL

35th International Annual Conference
Brighton, 17–21 April 2001

Edited by Alan Pulverness

Editorial Committee: Jonathan Marks, Jacky Newbrook, Amos Paran

This publication sponsored by

UNIVERSITY *of* CAMBRIDGE
Local Examinations Syndicate

iatefl

Published by IATEFL, 3 Kingsdown Chambers,
Kingsdown Park, Whitstable, Kent CT5 2DJ

First published 2001

British Library Cataloguing in Publication Data
Education
Pulverness, Alan (Ed.)
IATEFL 2001 Brighton Conference Selections

ISBN 1 901095 01 0

For a complete list of IATEFL publications, please write to the above address, or visit the IATEFL website at www.iatefl.org

IATEFL Publications Officer: Jonathan Marks. Copy-edited by Sue Harmes.
Designed and typeset by Keith Rigley, Charlbury.
Printed in Britain by Information Press, Eynsham.

CONTENTS

EDITOR'S INTRODUCTION

For its *35th International Annual Conference*, the IATEFL returned to the Brighton Conference Centre for the first time since 1997. Brighton, selected as the biennial conference venue for the next few years, should properly be called Brighton and Hove. However, residents of Hove have tended to disassociate themselves from Brighton, so that the more respectable end of the city is sometimes known as 'Hove Actually' (as in 'I live in Hove, actually'). Beyond the confines of the conference centre, delegates were able to enjoy what the Brighton and Hove tourist guide website describes as 'its cosmopolitan air, oodles of restaurants, feverish nightlife and abundance of culture'.

For the last few years, the conference programme has reflected the increasing significance of information and communications technology (ICT), and in 2000 the Dublin conference had been enhanced by a virtual event on the Internet. This year the actual conference was again notable for two major technological innovations: the videoconference that made it possible for Carol A Chapelle to deliver the opening Plenary live from Iowa State University – and to interact with questioners from the floor in Brighton – and the Internet café, sponsored by Longman, which drew a steady stream of surfers to the exhibition hall. Screen addicts were able to surf the Net and keep up with e-mail correspondence, while one delegate, a tutor at a 'virtual university' based in Argentina, was able to drop into the café during the conference to run virtual seminars online.

Despite several breaks in transmission, Carol Chapelle retained her composure and her patience throughout, giving an authoritative overview of the pedagogical capabilities of ICT, which should have proved persuasive to any doubting technophobes in the audience. The text of her talk is reproduced in Chapter 1, together with the transcript of the question-and-answer sessions which punctuated the Plenary. The event had something of the experimental flavour of Logie Baird's first television transmissions, and though the technology is still in its infancy, given the speed with which ICT applications are developing, by the time of the York conference in 2002, we may well be looking back on the tentative quality of this year's videoconference with some incredulity.

The *Conference Selections* are framed, as the conference was itself, by the opening and closing Plenaries. On the final morning in Brighton, Professor David Crystal, IATEFL's patron, brought us full circle, with a comprehensive account (Chapter 9) of the effects that ICT is having on the language. Professor Crystal's virtuoso talk identified a dizzying range of neologisms, emoticons, and deviant spelling and punctuation, analysing and classifying language phenomena that are evolving as fast as the technology that is producing them. One of the functions of the *Selections* is to inform members who were unable to attend the conference, and Professor Crystal's catalogue of Netspeak is likely to be such an invaluable resource for teachers, as well as language analysts, that we felt it should be reproduced in full.

The other talking point of this year's conference was undoubtedly the debate on the future of global English, jointly sponsored by Macmillan Heinemann and the *Guardian Weekly* (see Chapter 5). Chaired by Will Hutton, author of *The State We're In* and editor of *The Observer*, the debate featured challenging talks by Robert Phillipson and John Walsh on equal language rights and the future of minority languages, and by Juliane House, Barbara Seidlhofer and Jennifer Jenkins on English as a European *lingua franca*.

The texts of these talks appeared in the *Guardian Weekly* in April to coincide with the debate, but again we felt that this year's *Selections* would provide an incomplete record of the conference if the debate were not represented. We are grateful to the *Guardian Weekly* for supplying the texts.

The *International Annual Conference* reflects the very wide range of pedagogic and research activity of the Association's members, and this year is no exception. Chapter 2, *Approaches and methods*, opens with three reports by David Killick, Rob Batstone and Eleanor Watts, which challenge some of the underlying assumptions of the communicative consensus, in terms of cross-cultural capability, psycholinguistic processes and appropriate methodology. There is also a report by Graham Hall of a panel discussion on the 'pedagogy of bare essentials', which reflected on a year in the life of the 'Dogme' group. Inspired by Scott Thornbury's ELT 'vow of chastity' (in *IATEFL Issues* 153) and by the *Dogme 95* group of Danish film-makers, the ELT Dogme group have likewise eschewed 'razzmatazz and special effects' in the classroom, opting for a low-tech methodology that privileges the emergent language of the learner. The rest of this chapter includes reports on the development of individual language skills, on testing and exam preparation, and on the use of drama, art and film. The chapter closes with the first of two joint Plenary papers: Susan Stempleski and Barry Tomalin's history of ELT film and video, which also identifies some current and future directions for these media.

Robin Walker, whose report opens Chapter 3, was one of several presenters who addressed the issue of 'pronunciation goals' in the light of Jennifer Jenkins' work on English as a *lingua franca*. Other reports in this chapter deal with pedagogic applications of conversational analysis, corpus data and research into memory and comprehension, as well as other areas of language and learning, such as communication strategies, literacy and translation. The two final short reports in this chapter, from Antoinette Moses and Andrew Walkley, address language issues that are often neglected – or shunned – in the classroom: cliché and swearing. Chapter 3 closes with Kari Smith's Plenary paper on *Children's rights, assessment and the digital portfolio*. Drawing on key principles set out in the United Nations Convention on the Rights of the Child, Kari illustrated the concept of the digital portfolio with a vivid example of a process 'dialogue' conducted via computer with a ten-year-old learner. This was also a rare instance of a presentation whose use of PowerPoint was fully justified, though we are sadly unable to reproduce Kari's graphics in full colour.

Chapter 4, *Language in the classroom*, includes reports on a number of innovative teaching ideas which rely either on 'poor' technology (Elizabeth McMahon and Maria Heron's 'Grammarbox') or on the human resources of teacher and learners and the language that they use. Among the latter there are valuable reminders of what can be achieved through reformulation of learners' output, judicious use of the mother tongue, creative adaptations of substitution drills and focusing on the informal social interactions that take place 'before and after lessons, and during the break'.

The title of Chapter 6, *Focus on the learner*, might raise expectations of familiar accounts of research into learning styles and strategies, and proposals for appropriate learner training and awareness-raising. In fact, the research projects reported by Iphigenia Mahili and Maria de los Angeles Clemente in their respective presentations raise some important questions about diversity of strategy use, which should serve to modify some widely held assumptions about the nature of learner autonomy and self-directed learning. This chapter also features a report by Richard Masterson on aptitude, an area that receives rather little attention, as well as further reports on vocabulary guessing strategies and the use of fiction written for EFL learners. The chapter concludes with Grethe Hooper Hansen's Plenary paper on *Hemisphericity*. Most teachers will be aware of the division of the upper brain into left and right hemispheres, and of the broad division of their functions. Adopting Carla Hannaford's terminology of 'logic' (left hemisphere) and 'Gestalt' (right hemisphere), Grethe's paper provides a detailed account of hemisphericity, and discusses the implications for teaching of subtle variations in individuals' 'preferred dominance'.

The issue of world varieties of English in relation to pre-service training is addressed by Sebastian Watkins and Frances Hughes in the first report in Chapter 7. Other training and development topics dealt with in this chapter include the integration of task-based learning as an effective paradigm on training courses, the paradoxical reality of accommodating experienced teachers on pre-service courses, and lesson planning as a teacher development tool. Five of the eleven short reports in this chapter are concerned with classroom research, observation and feedback, and the final report, from Jonathan Gore, broadens the notion of teacher development to consider the situation of teachers who are promoted out of the classroom into management posts. The chapter closes with the second of this year's two joint Plenary papers: Gabriela Matei and Péter Medgyes' investigation of *Teaching as a political act*. Based on extensive research carried out by e-mail before the conference, this presentation identified teachers' attitudes and opinions in three 'political' domains: global English, teacher power and the status of teachers of English. The sub-title of the paper describes it as 'a non-PC dialogue', but only the video recording will do justice to the dialogic qualities of the live event!

Chapter 8 returns to the theme of ICT, and the range and diversity of applications discussed, including Web skills, CD-ROMs, electronic dictionaries, office software and electronic discussion boards, exemplifies many of the points outlined by Carol Chapelle.

The high standard of presentations at this year's conference was perhaps due to the new requirement to submit a 250-word abstract, together with the brief summary for the conference programme. This also seems to have prompted a much higher number of presenters to submit written reports for these proceedings. The editorial committee have had the invidious task of selecting fewer than half of the 125 reports received, and we have been forced by limitations of space to exclude many very worthwhile submissions. While *Selections* will continue to be published in book form for the foreseeable future, the answer perhaps lies in cyberspace: a number of presenters have already published their papers in full on the Internet, either in e-journals or on their own homepages. One presenter, James Chamberlain, preferred to publish electronically, and his paper (*Getting started in intercultural communication training*) can be accessed at http://www.spz.fh-rhein-sieg.de/english/iatefl/getting_started_iatefl.html. By the time we compile next year's *Selections*, we may well need to include a list of website addresses.

A final word of thanks to the editorial committee, Jacky Newbrook, Amos Paran and Jonathan Marks, and to copy editor Sue Harmes, for all their hard work.

Alan Pulverness
Norwich Institute for Language Education, August 2001

1 OPENING PLENARY

ELT, technology and change

Carol A Chapelle *Iowa State University, USA*

The turn of the century seems to be a natural time for looking to the future of our profession, and any discussion of the future implicates technology in one form or another. The members of IATEFL can get a glimpse of the technological future and some of the issues it raises in the papers included on the CD-ROM that resulted from the ESADE/IATEFL conference on *CALL in the 21st Century* in July 2000 in Barcelona. The special topic issue of *TESOL Quarterly* in 2000 also looks to the future of ELT with a focus on technology. These sources provide good starting points for considering some of the changes in ELT that have been prompted by the spread of technology throughout society. Most of the authors in these volumes view technology as a resource for learners and teachers. How does technology act as a resource, and what are the implications of this resource for the profession of ELT?

1 Technology as a resource

Technology acts as a resource within our context of culture, context of situation and linguistic system (Halliday & Hasan 1989). It affects the context of culture by amplifying particular aspects of culture, such as the value placed on information that is characteristic of western culture. It changes cultures by connecting members of different cultures, and it creates new cultures that exist in cyberspace – cultures with values and norms of their own. Technology affects field, tenor, and mode within the context of situation. In other words, our use of technology affects what we do, who we do it with, and how we use language to accomplish it. Bruce and Hogan (1998) point out in their paper, *The Disappearance of Technology*, that as technologies become embedded in our everyday context of situation, we cease to notice them altogether. At the linguistic level, technology affects many of the choices that we make. Murray (2000) explains that the linguistic choices users make as they engage in technology-mediated communication are different than those they make elsewhere. Narrowing our view of the changing world of technology down to our immediate concerns, we need to ask what these societal changes prompted by technology mean for ESL learners and teachers.

2 Implications of technology for ESL/EFL learners

For ESL students, new technologies have meant increased opportunity for using English and increased access to English-using speech communities that make use of technology. However, using English through technology may also imply the need for new skills.

Opportunities for using English

Lam (2000) provides an in-depth look at how the ESL learners she studied were afforded opportunities for successful use of English through technology. She wrote the following about an ESL learner in the US:

> After attending an introductory class on e-mail and browsing for information on the Web in a high school from which he would soon graduate, he continued to look up websites for tutorials on how to make personal home pages and conduct online chat. By Fall 1997, when he began his studies at a local Junior College, he had almost completed a personal homepage on a Japanese pop singer, had compiled a long list of online chatmates in several countries around the world, and was starting to write regularly to a few e-mail pals. (Lam 2000: 467)

Lam noticed the changes that these opportunities for using English through the Internet had prompted for this student. Before he got involved in his Internet community, he felt overwhelmed, saying 'English is my biggest problem. It's like this place, the United States, isn't my world ... My English won't be that good, even in ten years.' She noticed that after he had spent two years working with these communities online, his observations were very different. He reported: 'Now I feel there's nothing much to be afraid of ... It was my Internet friends who helped me to change and encouraged me.' (Lam 2000: 467–468) He attributed the improvement in his English and in his outlook to his use of English on the Internet. An important part of this process was the fact that this learner could find a group with whom he could communicate about a topic that he was interested in.

Access to English-using speech communities

The concept of 'speech community' is important, as we look at the new forms of communication available on the Internet. Murray defines a speech community as 'a group of people who share linguistic and non-linguistic interaction but whose norms may be evolving or may be the site of struggle. The language of CMC [Computer-Mediated Communication] exhibits certain characteristics and speech communities have incorporated this new medium into their repertoire of language use in particular ways' (2000: 399).

It is difficult to estimate the extent to which English learners around the world have access to and take advantage of such English-using speech communities on the Internet. Some data indicate that access is more and more available. For example, Cyberatlas, on the Internet, has statistics about who is using the Internet, and front-page items pertaining to ESL learners can be found regularly on this site. According to this source, 'more than half of Chinese-Americans have Internet access, and almost all of them own a PC' and 'there is more evidence that the digital divide in America may be closing, especially among the young Hispanic community' (*The Big Picture Demographics*, April 10, 2001).

In a study done several years ago, Taylor, Jamieson and Eignor (2000) looked at computer use by TOEFL takers all around the world. Overall, there were very few (5.9%) learners in this group who had never used a computer. The number of learners who had used a computer once week or more, or who had used the computer a fair amount, was about 70%. Although these results would be stronger today, in 1997 many learners internationally were already using the Internet. A point that should be noticed, though, is that there was a large amount of regional variation. Many learners find access and opportunities to use computers, whereas other learners do not.

Communicative competence with technology

The prevalence of opportunities for participation in communication through technology suggests the need for acquiring communicative competence with technology. Cox and de

Assis-Peterson (1999) present a fascinating quote from a teacher, collected during interviews in which teachers of English in Brazil were asked to talk about English language teaching and how it fitted into their world, and their students' world. The teacher said: 'There are three kinds of illiterate people in the world, the one who does not know how to read or write, the one who does not know how to use a computer, and the one who does not know English.' This shows her perceptions of the needs of the learners include English *and* technology.

Some argue that it is in learners' interest to combine the two, and therefore combining technology and English is the current challenge for English teachers. Warschauer (2000) suggests that new language and literacy skills are needed for effective communication and that the concept of reading and writing skills be replaced by the broader abilities he calls reading/research and writing/authorship. These terms make sense in the light of Rassool's (1999) definition of communicative competence in the twenty-first century. She points out

> in a world increasingly driven by (a) the need for innovation through research and development (R&D), (b) the multilevelled changes brought about in our everyday lives as a result of the nature and speed of technological developments, (c) the volume and range of information available, and its open accessibility, (d) the multimodal features of electronic text as well as (e) its interactive nature, we require significantly *more* than just the ability to read and write in a functional way.
>
> (Rassool 1999: 202; emphasis in original)

This characterization of the context of culture and situation in the twenty-first century forces us to look more carefully at the view of communicative competence that has been useful in language teaching and assessment. The context of situation is always connected to and affects the nature of the language knowledge and the world knowledge that are needed in any particular situation. We need to think about how the addition of technology to the context of situation will affect the definition of communicative competence. What does it mean for the additional kinds of strategies that must be a part of strategic competence? What does it mean for aspects of language knowledge or aspects of pragmatics for coping and dealing with a variety of technology-mediated situations? What does this mean about the technology-related world knowledge that is needed for communication today?

Questions and answers on ESL learners and technology

Q: *In your experience, what are most EFL teachers' reactions to modern technology? Are they comfortable with it? Do they feel threatened by it? Do they know how to make it work for them instead of feeling intimidated by it?*

A: It is difficult to answer in a categorical way. Obviously, as a profession, we are very diverse in knowledge, interests, aspirations and skills. Many of the language teachers I work with are very interested in using technology, but typically do not feel completely comfortable with it or competent with it. Even all of us who have worked with technology quite a bit are always finding that the changes continue to be very challenging, so a part of our careers these days is to continue learning more about technology.

Q: *Do you consider Educational Technology a real innovation in mainstream educational development deeply rooted in educational research, or just a twenty-first century cybermania?*

A: We are seeing both in educational technology, but it is probably not really within our choice to consider it as a mania that will go away and will not really affect us.

Q: *We all know that technology is a very good tool to help people learn a foreign language, English in particular, but I would like to point out that in some places, it is difficult to get the technology. Is there any chance through UNESCO or any other organization that some centres will help to utilize this technology?*

A: That is a good question. I would add that things are changing so fast that keeping up with the technology is very difficult in every setting, developed or less-developed countries.

Q: *In what ways have you had to adapt or restrict your own lecture today for using this medium? In other words, what qualities in your normal lecturing mode are we missing right now?*

A: I probably would have used more technology if I were there in Brighton. The overall style is not radically different.

Q: *What effect does using the Internet and e-mail have on the language itself?*[1]

A: That is a really interesting and important area for research and there are some people investigating it. Murray (2000) looks at the particular characteristics of registers that have developed within electronic communication. It is a good topic.

Q: *If, as predicted, Chinese becomes the language of the Internet in the future, what implications does this hold for the English language?*

A: That would have some implications. I haven't thought that one through. That issue has not crossed my mind, but I think I should think about it further.

Q: *How we can turn the idea of communicative competence into being part of technological competence when most of our English language examinations do not take this into consideration?*

A: There are two ways of taking technology into account in English examinations. One is simply delivering exams on computers, and many of the large companies are doing that. ETS is doing that with the TOEFL. Cambridge deliver many of their exams on computer, or are moving in that direction. The other way is asking ourselves how we should be testing language differently because of the combination of language and technology skills that we are interested in. This is an issue that has not been explored thoroughly.

Q: *How wide is the use of videoconferencing for the purposes of English teaching and learning in the United States, and what sort of companies provide this?*

A: I am afraid I do not know. I do not have a good answer to that. My sense is that it is not very widely used, in part because in the US, there is not that much need to videoconference in English because English is everywhere already. So the need may not be as great for that market to develop it at this time. Obviously videoconferencing is not everyday technology at this point, but with the development of the Internet, it will be in the future.

Q: *You have been talking about technology for communicative acts, e-mail, chat, distance communication. What do you see as the role of language learning multi-media packages either on the Web or on CD-ROM?*

A: We have that as another option. Teachers certainly have access to a lot of materials.

3 Implications for ESL teachers

As ESL teachers, what kind of resources does technology make available for us? Just as the changes in technology imply differences in learners' abilities, so do they imply the need for teachers to develop new skills? Teachers have had and will continue to have strong feelings about technology. Cummins (2000) points out that it is important that teachers view technology as a resource.

> Rather than dismissing IT as another corporate plot, as many critical educators have tended to do, or lamenting its perverse impact on educational priorities, we should acknowledge the fundamental changes that IT is bringing to our societies and seek ways to use its power for transformative purposes.
>
> (Cummins 2000: 539)

Four examples show how technology can be considered as a resource for ELT: computer-assisted corpus linguistics, focusing on form, tasks for negotiation of meaning, and observation of learners.

Computer-assisted corpus linguistics

Corpus linguists use electronically stored texts and computer programs that search and count grammatical features to study language. Conrad (2000) identifies three important influences on language teaching of this method of linguistic analysis, the first of which is that 'monolithic descriptions of English grammar will be replaced by register-specific descriptions,' a fact that has implications for language teaching. Conrad presents the example of linking adverbials (e.g. *but*, *however*, *therefore*) and how they are used across three registers: conversation, news reportage, academic language. Conrad points out that particular adverbials are chosen with different frequencies depending on the register of language use, and therefore that adverbials should be introduced and practised in view of the registers in which they are actually used. A second influence Conrad (2000) predicts is that that the teaching of grammar will become more integrated with the teaching of vocabulary. She presents examples of the way in which verb complements are chosen by different verbs:

a) 'Everyone says to eat vegetables.'
b) 'Everyone says that you should eat vegetables.'

Both sentences are grammatically correct, since the verb *say* can have a *to*-complement or a *that*-complement. The work in corpus linguistics, however, provides better information than what is grammatically correct: it tells us which complements are actually chosen with the greater frequency by proficient English users. For the example above, *that*-complements are more frequently used with *say*. So, what do we want to teach, considering that the large majority of times students will come across and need to use *that*-complements?

A third influence Conrad (2000) predicts is that the focus of grammar teaching will change from structural accuracy to appropriate conditions of use. The two sentences presented below are examples of grammatically correct sentences used in different situations:

a) 'It should be recognized, however, that not everyone wishes to display power.'

b) 'That not everyone wishes to display power should be recognized.'

Again, here, the fact that the two syntactic structures are possible in English is far less useful to the learner than the fact the structure in example (a) is more frequently used.

These insights coming from computer-assisted corpus linguistics studies – the importance of register, the importance of lexis, the importance of appropriate use – have been important for changing the profession's view of grammar, and how it should be taught.

Focusing on form

A second way of considering technology as a resource derives from the report of Doug Mills (2000) on software tools that allow teachers to focus learners' attention on linguistic form. Let's consider the following text for ESL learners from an example that can be found on the Web (Chapelle 1997):

> 'I'm not going to beat around the bush,' announced J.D. Jacobson, head of the marketing division ... Daniel Burson, on the other hand, knew that foreign languages were not at all up his alley.

In this particular text, there are a couple of American idioms and a pedagogical strategy for teaching them. Doug Mills (2000) points out that software tools allow for marking up a text in a way that indicates where the idioms are, thus drawing the learner's attention to the form. On the web browser, the idiom would appear in italics as follows:

> 'I'm not going to <I>beat around the bush<I>', announced J.D. Jacobson, head of the marketing division ... Daniel Burson, on the other hand, knew that foreign languages were not at all <I>up his alley<I>.

Another program exists – a style sheet – that may interpret the mark-up for the idiom in a variety of ways. In the example above, one of the idioms is a verbal construction and the other is a predicate adjective construction. So, we could add <V> and <PA> to <I>. Once a text is marked up, the program will allow for showing the various grammatical forms in different ways.

These are just a couple of examples of the ways in which text mark-up languages or style sheets can produce displays focusing on particular linguistic features. There are comparable audio and video programs, some of them already implemented in CD-ROM packages. In sum, there are software tools that provide mechanisms for drawing learners' attention to form, according to recent research, a requisite for acquiring a language.

Tasks for negotiation of meaning

A third way of looking at technology as a resource results from the fact that the Internet provides new tools for producing second language tasks. Looking back at the kinds of language learning tasks used for many years in the classroom, traditional ones were usually based on the textbooks or the realia brought in to class. They tended to deal with oral face-to-face language and be carried out with familiar classmates in a classroom. Tasks developed though the Internet provide new features, new values for field, tenor, mode. The topics that can be discussed are information and opinions, but also news and discussion of specific topics through bulletin boards. Participants in these activities can consist of not only familiar classmates, but also unfamiliar ones in other countries. The communication can consist of both written and oral language interaction.

Observation of learners

A fourth way in which technology acts as a resource for ELT is by providing a record of what the learner is doing, so that teachers have a means of looking at the learners' interactions while working with materials. Learner–computer interaction gets reported and allows us to look at the extent to which learners use resource materials available on the CD-ROM, or the extent to which they used the review materials that were provided. Learner–learner interactions through written communication can be recorded for teachers to examine and use in subsequent teaching. These are the options available with the new technologies that are of interest to English teachers who are prepared to work with data concerning learners' language (Chapelle 2001).

4 Technology and teacher education

Given these potential resources, it is necessary to face the question of how they can be put into practice. This brings up the question of what teachers need to know to use these technologies in their classrooms. Kamhi-Stein (2000) observed a TESOL methods course, where the students (future ESL teachers) used interactive bulletin boards to a large extent. Based on her observations she suggested that 'if ESL teachers are to use technology effectively for teaching in the future, they must use it for learning while they are students. Limiting technology experiences to one course or to one area of teacher preparation is insufficient for developing teachers who can use technology creatively and flexibly.'

Cummins (2000) points out that technology is part of the life that learners are preparing for, and as a consequence, it needs to serve as an integral part of teacher education. I would suggest that technology may be considered among the core areas of focus in ELT teacher education. In fact, it seems that much of what is taught about language might be done through technology, drawing on corpus linguistics in particular. This may be done if linguistics courses embrace the technologies available for developing and exploring patterns in language. Similarly, teacher education programmes might emphasize knowledge about language learning through technology. Also essential is the teaching of skills for using technology, as mentioned above. ELT professionals need strong technology skills, and therefore teacher education needs to prepare future and current teachers accordingly.

Questions and answers

Q: *There are a number of sites that allow the user to choose the language they want to use. Will English and the use of Internet in ESL teaching not decrease in importance as the number of multi-language sites increases?*

A: Yes. This is one of the stimulating issues we need to think about as language teachers. Cribb (2000) writes about the importance and the significance that machine translation is going to have for English language teaching. In reality, the scenario for our profession is not good because it suggested that the technologies for translation, not only on the Internet but for telephones for personal conversations, are going to advance so rapidly that people will not need to learn English any more!

Q: *In your view, has the increased use of CALL, computer-assisted language learning, and ICT, information and communications technology, in language teaching and language learning, provided any new insights into how language is learned?*

A: This is a good question. Those of us who are enthusiastic about technology need to take this question very seriously in order to ask what we, as technology users, can provide back to the rest of the profession. There are tools available at this point that might be used this way. There are, in particular, some studies of second language acquisition that have attempted to carefully control conditions of teaching and provide insights. There have been studies that investigate whether implicit versus explicit instruction works better. There have been ethnographic studies, such as Lam's (2000), that look at the literacy skills and again problematize the issue of context in communicative competence. All of these address this basic question, but ideally in the future these tiny contributions can be augmented.

Q: *How does technology influence testing? It seems there are too many itemized multiple choice questions in current computer testing.*

A: What we are experiencing with the first generation of computer-assisted tests, is not really all that technology can do. What people have done for operational tests, and for good reasons, has been very conservative in using the technology and has been very traditional in item format. The next generation may start making better use of the technology. It is likely that we will see online tests that take advantage of audio and video, that look at a variety of tasks that can be done in language testing, and that users can access for their own benefit. The largest and probably one of the most important projects in language testing is the DIALING project in Europe, which has produced tests that learners can use on their own even.

Q: *How can we remedy the fact that while institutions are prepared to give significant funding to hardware, there is often a reluctance to provide funding for the training of teachers to use this technology?*

A: This is one of the largest issues that the profession faces everywhere. The hardware exists, but the 'peopleware' (for training and support) doesn't. There are no easy solutions for this issue. We all face the same problems, so maybe there is the need for an international organization, since the needs are general and not local or individual.

Q: *Could you comment on how you or we together might raise the awareness of the importance and centrality of many of the issues you described today to the wider English language teaching community?*

A: This is a really important question that is beginning to be addressed. The teachers interested in technology and working in technology have tended to cluster in groups and develop their own professional organizations and journals. But more and more, the issues of technology are facing everyone. Teachers need to be using technology in all the classes, not only in the computer-assisted language learning class.

Q: *Learning a language is a human activity, and language is a human device, and in two respects it looks as if the human dimension is being left out. Are we missing the human dimension by focusing on technology?*

A: I think we could, but at the same time technology is very much impacting and working together with humanity. It's very much a part of our communication system in the modern world, and I think people see that differently depending on their point of view and perspective. This question again underscores the context of culture and the differing roles of technology across different cultures.

Note

[1] See Chapter 9 for David Crystal's account of the linguistic changes being wrought by ICT.

References

Bachman L F (1990) *Fundamental considerations in language testing.* Oxford: Oxford University Press

Bruce B C & M P Hogan (1998) The disappearance of technology: Toward an ecological model of literacy. In *Handbook of literacy and technology: Transformations in a post-typographic world* (pp. 269–281). Mahwah, NJ: Lawrence Erlbaum Associates

Chapelle C A (2001) *Computer applications in second language acquisition: Foundations for teaching, testing and research.* Cambridge: Cambridge University Press

Chapelle C A (1997) CALL in the year 2000: Still in search of research agendas? In *Language Learning and Technology, 1 (1)*, 19–43. Available at http://llt.msu.edu/vol1num1/chapelle/default.html

Conrad S (2000) Will corpus linguistics revolutionize grammar teaching in the 21st century? In *TESOL Quarterly, 34(3)*, 548–560

Cox M I P & A A de Assis-Peterson (1999) Critical pedagogy in ELT: Images of Brazilian teachers of English. In *TESOL Quarterly, 33(3)*, 433–452

Cribb V M (2000) Machine translation: The alternative for the 21st Century? In *TESOL Quarterly, 34(3)*, 560–569

Cummins J (2000) Academic language learning, transformative pedagogy, and information technology: towards a critical balance. In *TESOL Quarterly, 34(3)*, 537–548

CyberAtlas (2001) *The big picture demographics*. Retrieved April 10, 2001, from the World Wide Web: http://cyberatlas.internet.com/big_picture/demographics

Halliday M A K & R Hasan (1989) *Language, context, and text: aspects of language in a social-semiotic perspective.* Oxford: Oxford University Press

Hawisher G E & C L Self (Eds.) (2000) *Global literacies and the World-Wide Web.* London: Routledge

Ioannou-Georgiou S (2000) Researching computer-mediated communication. In Brett P (Ed.) *CALL in the 21st century*. CD-ROM published by ESADE/IATEFL

Kamhi-Stein L D (2000) Looking to the future of TESOL teacher education: Web-based bulletin board discussions in a methods course. In *TESOL Quarterly, 34(3)*, 423–455

Kern R (2000) *Literacy and language teaching*. Oxford: Oxford University Press

Lam W S E (2000) L2 literacy and the design of the self: A case study of a teenager writing on the Internet. In *TESOL Quarterly, 34(3)*, 457–482

Mills D (2000) Web-based technology as a resource for form-focused language learning. In *TESOL Quarterly, 34(3)*, 603–615

Murray D (2000) Protean communication: The language of computer-mediated communication. In *TESOL Quarterly, 34(3)*, 457–482

Pennington M (2000) Writing minds and talking fingers: Doing literacy in the electronic age. In Brett P (Ed.) *CALL in the 21st century*. CD-ROM published by ESADE/IATEFL

Rassool N (1999) *Literacy for sustainable development in the age of information.* Clevedon, UK: Multilingual Matters

Smith B & M J Alvarez-Torres (2000). Technology-influenced and learner-controlled factors in successful negotiation of meaning in task-based computer-mediated communication. In Brett P (Ed.) *CALL in the 21st century*. CD-ROM published by ESADE/IATEFL

Taylor C, J Jamieson & D Eignor (2000). Trends in computer use among international students. In *TESOL Quarterly, 34(3)*, 575–585

Warschauer M (2000) The changing global economy and the future of English teaching. In *TESOL Quarterly, 34*(3), 511–535

2 APPROACHES AND METHODS

2.1 Cross-cultural capability and communicative language teaching: Why the paradigm needs to shift

David Killick *Leeds Metropolitan University, England*

The paradigm shift which led us to embrace the communicative approach some decades ago, failed to take on board the major element of change implicit within the notion of communicative competence – a shift from the profession's enduring focus on language to a focus on the users of that language (both learner and proficient speaker).

Recent decades have seen the rise of a number of sub-disciplines within applied linguistics, each dedicated to the exploration of the minutiae of language systems or language processes. We all – teachers, researchers and publishers – feel rather comfortable with a communicative approach which continues to focus on (broadly) 'grammar'.

The communicative approach, though, requires us to recognise the reality that communication is a *cultural act*, and this means a social act, a 'between people' act. And what takes place in the space between is determined only partially by the vehicle of the language upon which meaning is transported; 'intercultural (communicative) competence is defined as the general linguistic, social and psychological abilities that make a successful interaction with individuals or groups from other cultures possible' (Moosmuller in Aarup Jensen et al 1995).

There is, then, a trinity of skills required for effective communicative competence: Linguistic, Psychological, Social. The real paradigm shift is to recognise the centrality of hitherto largely alien discipline areas such as social psychology, ethnography/anthropology and intercultural communication, to our field of operation. The boundaries we have created in our profession, through the exclusive alliance with the discipline of applied linguistics, are narrow and limiting. We need to embrace other areas to shape our discipline, a working title for which is *Cross-Cultural Capability*.

This is necessary in part because it is abundantly clear that despite the best efforts of an enormous research and publishing community, applied linguistics continues to fail to provide the theoretical models upon which we can fully develop a pedagogy which enables effective communicative competence in all its dimensions, and in part because the world, however much a cliché it may be, *is* rapidly becoming a 'global village'. Cross-cultural encounter, once limited to the wealthy or the dispossessed, is becoming a commonplace for most of the population of many countries, and the imperatives for understanding, tolerance and effective communication are upon us.

In seeking to achieve the capabilities to communicate across cultures, the outcome we are working towards is someone who can not only communicate within a limited range of cultures, but rather somebody able to communicate effectively in their target language whatever the cultural context:

> A key characteristic of intercultural competence is the fact that it prepares the learner for exposure to all cultures, not just the one whose language is being learned.
>
> (Murghan 1999)

E-mail: d.killick@lmu.ac.uk

2.2 Classroom culture and language learning

Rob Batstone *Institute of Education, England*

Communicative language teaching has become the orthodoxy. Yet for all its benefits, it is limited, inevitably, by its very nature. Such is its concern with the social discourse of competent language use, that it leaves largely unaccounted for the other side of the equation – the *psycho*linguistic contexts of language learning.

In this paper I attempted to give some substance to such a view by taking a particular definition of communicative language use and indicating aspects of language learning which fall outside its scope. The key ability in language use, Widdowson argues, is 'the ability to use a knowledge of language as a resource for the creation of meaning' (1983: 25), as when we use language to the degree necessary to get a point over in debate, or when reading a passage for information.

But the 'least effort' principle implicit in this view of language means that learners can often circumvent the need to attend very much to language, yet still get the business done. Mindful of such problems, many scholars have looked for a communicative solution to this most communicative of difficulties, by constructing texts where the language necessary to complete the task is also the language which learners have no communicative option but to attend to. The following sentence – taken from a study by Cadierno (1995) – illustrates where learners have to read a series of sentences, indicating whether present or past time is referred to:

1 Antonio called his parents on the phone.

Notice that the 'least effort' principle cannot be put into effect here because there are no clues signalling past time except the grammar itself, so that the learner is *compelled* to heed it, through what is called 'bottom up' processing.

Very neat, but there's a catch: if the learners *already know* the past tense, then all well and good. But if they don't, then all we have done is remove from the context the very cues which they need. In example 2 such a cue is deliberately provided (the phrase 'three days ago'), thus giving the learner a point of reference from which to go on to make sense of the target grammar:

2 Antonio called his parents on the phone **three days ago**.

Of course a strictly communicative user might get as far as the lexical phrase and stop right there, further exploration being redundant. But language learners need to operationalize a different principle, taking advantage of the lexis in 2 as a *resource* with which to make sense of the target grammar. This reverses the direction of flow outlined by Widdowson, for rather than using prior knowledge of grammar as a resource to make meaning, the learner here is *learning how to* make meaning, a process which itself needs to be resourced through the careful construction of contextual cues.

Ultimately learners do indeed need to become communicatively adept. But to get there they need resourcing contexts of a very different kind.

2.3 Missionary or teacher? The communicative language teacher outside Europe

Eleanor Watts *Freelance, England*

The communicative approach has blossomed where it evolved, in Europe, North America and Australia. But the vast majority of people learning English live in Asia, Africa and South America. Over the past twenty years, evangelistic English teachers – like me – have tried with missionary zeal to sow the seeds of communicative language teaching in developing countries. Like many missionaries, some of us have come to see that these seeds may not flourish in different soils.

The workshop participants were first asked to get into groups for an information gap exercise, an activity popular with communicative language teachers. They then discussed the difficulties they would have in implementing this activity with a class of eighty children. Both practical and cultural problems were raised. They were invited to imagine themselves in the following teaching conditions, grading those that presented the greatest obstacles to communicative language teaching:

a) There are eighty children in each class.
b) There is no wall between your class and the class next door.
c) Your school provides no card, scissors, felt-tips or drawing pins.
d) Materials are vulnerable to damp, goats and white ants.
e) English is assessed only by students' knowledge of set texts and grammar.
f) The syllabus is heavy, so there is little time for talk.
g) You have no access to photocopiers, videos, tape-recorders, OHPs or a library.
h) Your own English is not fluent.
i) Your society believes that learning comes from the teacher, not the pupils.

Interestingly, the group had very different answers, variously listing a, b, e, f, g, h and i as the greatest obstacles for the communicative approach. I then suggested that the following approaches were most practical in the above conditions:

- Teachers should choose games which involve no expensive, easily lost cards or slips of paper.
- Teacher-led activities are easier to manage and culturally more acceptable than pupil-led activities.
- Open-ended discussion can be encouraged in class, but needs to be limited in writing, because of the marking load on teachers.
- Pairwork is preferable to groupwork as it involves less movement and noise.

While we can adapt the communicative approach to the context in which we teach, Holliday (1994) and Canagarajah (1999) ask how far it is appropriate to use it at all. This methodology emerged in a culture where the teacher could be viewed as a facilitator who enables students to express their own ideas. But in many cultures, the teacher is regarded as the source of sacred knowledge, which is passed down to obedient pupils. Accuracy is traditionally prized over fluency. Product is regarded as more important than process. Games are seen as trivializing the serious business of education. Co-operative learning is regarded as poor preparation for a competitive society.

Canagarajah (1999) quotes a student who said, 'These new methods are constructed with western students in mind. Because our culture is different, they are irrelevant to our concerns.' We would be ostriches if we did not at least wonder whether his student was right.

E-mail: wattsele@cs.com

2.4 Dogme ELT: For a pedagogy of bare essentials

Graham Hall *University of Northumbria, England*

A year ago, Scott Thornbury invited ELT teachers, trainers and writers to join him in his ELT 'vow of chastity' (Thornbury 2000). By analogy, he adopted the principles (and name) of the Danish *Dogme 95* film-makers, who sought to restore a concern for the 'inner life' of characters rather than razzmatazz and special effects. His call struck a chord with the other members of what became an active e-mail discussion group, in which EFL teachers/professionals have explored the possibilities of teaching in the spirit of *dogme* – not a 'method', let alone a 'dogma'; more a state of mind.

A year of talking, teaching and training later, the panel, all active members of the *dogme* group, came to present our case. We had three aims – to try to summarise a year of both theoretical and practical discussion; to show, using practical examples, how this affected our own teaching; and to give the audience time to talk and to talk back.

Summarising the year, we argued that ELT is currently in danger of becoming swamped by materials and technology, and that the only resources the teacher really needs to mediate successful learning can be found within themselves and their learners. As a result, the time has come to promote a 'poor' methodology, unshackled from the grammar treadmill, stripped of special effects, grounded in the local and relevant concerns of the people in the room. Giving first-hand accounts about our own very different teaching environments, we showed how these principles have been implemented in a variety of contexts, from a Polish paint factory to a British university. We emphasised the idea that lessons and language can 'emerge' from the people in the classroom – from their 'inner lives'.

A short 'back of the envelope' dictation and subsequent 'conversation' about the kind of personal experience from which language can emerge provided the audience with a concrete example of a short *dogme*-style practical activity. Talking back, the audience raised a number of questions. Did sentences scribbled before the session constitute materials? If not, what exactly did we mean by 'materials'? Were we referring only to published materials? Did students without materials feel short-changed? Is *dogme* really appropriate in all contexts? Does *dogme* lead to more language learning?

In response, we re-emphasised the *dogme* group's focus on 'learners' rather than 'materials' – that we were not so much 'materials minus' as 'learners plus', reaching our conclusion that perhaps 'less is more' when it comes to allowing the people in the classroom to explore and exploit their full potential. Finally, we invited the audience to join our e-mail discussion (http://groups.yahoo.com/group/dogme), and to try *dogme* approaches in their teaching for 15 minutes, a lesson, or a week in their own local contexts.

The whole session was 'organised' within the spirit of *dogme*. People communicated, sometimes heatedly, about what we said. Sometimes the discussion went where we had hoped; sometimes it went to places that we hadn't anticipated. But it always visited people's own teaching experiences and contexts. And there were no handouts.

E-mail: g.hall@unn.ac.uk

2.5 Four legs good, two legs better?

Simon Gill *Olomouc University, Czech Republic*

Communicative approaches to language teaching, despite their popularity during the last twenty years and the methodological advances associated with them, have often tended to belittle or even to ignore the cultural baggage that learners and users of English invariably bring with them to any context in which they use the language, and which, a growing body of evidence suggests, has a major influence on the quality and effectiveness of communication. This is, I would suggest, a serious defect, and one that I feel can in large part be addressed by enriching ELT through the introduction of elements of *intercultural learning.* This is an area which I have become increasingly convinced in recent years is a key one.

The presentation took the form of a workshop at which participants were invited to participate in a sequence of practical 'hands-on' activities that had already seen the light of day in various classrooms I have taught in. They were selected for the purpose of illustrating a number of principles that I believe can justify and underpin the introduction of intercultural learning in the ELT classroom:

- Communication does not take place in a cultural vacuum but a cultural context.
- Language and culture are intimately bound up together.
- Cultures are not monolithic.
- Individual identity is multi-faceted.
- Given the global role of English, familiarity with 'native speaker' norms of language and culture is increasingly seldom likely to be adequate.
- Facts alone are not enough; skills are of greater significance.
- It is crucial to try to objectify both the familiar and the unfamiliar.
- It is essential to get away from stock images and stereotypes; this may mean confronting them.
- It is important to compare and contrast.
- Individual insights and experience are important.
- 'Ordinary' things are of real interest.
- The relationship of the general and the specific is vital.
- An element of discovery learning is essential.
- We need to keep in mind broader educational principles (e.g. notions of lifelong education, empowerment) and do more than pay lip service to them.
- Dimensions such as the European and the global are important.
- Ultimately, *what* we deal with is less significant than *how* we deal with it.

The activities themselves included:

- a discussion of which end participants preferred to open bananas
- a worksheet-based activity concerned with notions of 'normality'

- a look at *symbols* and what they stand for, through the example of paper money
- looking at a poem that dealt with stereotypes
- language and cultural work based on a student's essay about her home country

Unfortunately, the limited space available does not permit a more detailed description. However, these activities, and more, as well as other materials pertaining to this area (such as articles, a bibliography and links) can be found described in greater detail on the following website: http://members.tripod.com/simonmgill/index.html

E-mail: pangill@hotmail.com

2.6 Learning to listen or listening to learn?

Richard Side *The Eckersley School of English, England*

Why, I wondered, have I felt such unease with what appears to be the industry standard way of dealing with listening? I observe these lessons, see them in coursebooks, occasionally even teach them myself: you listen to a recording (scripted, and often poorly acted) twice, listen for gist, listen for some specific points, and then discuss the subject matter. The discussion seems to be the ultimate aim of these lessons. The recording does not do much more than provide a topic to discuss. Tasks are information-based. Students listen to glean information. Then they give their opinions. Rarely in these lessons are many areas of language discussed. Teachers, for instance, seem reluctant to spend time analyzing and pinpointing possible reasons for incomprehension or misunderstanding – was it unknown words, or known words not recognised at speed, or syntax, or simply that the speakers were speaking too fast for the listener to process the information in time? This reluctance is perhaps perfectly understandable: apart from the technical problem of finding the place on the cassette which can help to solve the misunderstanding, even if you can find it quickly, it is often extremely difficult and time-consuming to pinpoint the cause of the problem accurately and, most importantly, *usefully*. Far better just to tell them what the answer is and race on to the all-important discussion.

So whereas in a reading lesson, or writing lesson, or vocabulary lesson, or whatever, there is (one hopes) a clear purpose – that the learner will leave the lesson better equipped in the future to deal with an area of language with greater competence than before – with the listening lesson, they merely leave better informed about train timetables, or pollution, or somebody else's funny experience. The language, it seems to be tacitly assumed, will be absorbed by some sort of vague osmosis. Somehow, some of it will just stick. The comprehension questions focus on understanding this particular recording, not on increasing one's ability to listen in general. They are a *test* of listening comprehension rather than a tool for learning. Apart, that is, from the more general 'learning strategies': predicting what is going to be said, learning to cope with not understanding everything, trying to grasp the gist, hanging on in there hoping that you'll get back on track in a moment. Strategies, in other words, that teach you how to deal with *in*comprehension, rather than stretching your ability to comprehend. Communicative (coping) strategies rather than learning strategies.

In my talk, I outlined some tasks that help learners to focus on the language problems involved in listening. Some recent published materials seem now to be including more structured language-based tasks. The dissatisfaction I describe above seems to have been felt also by others and the industry standard is evolving. There is, it seems, more willingness on the part of materials writers to tackle head-on the linguistic problems learners have with listening, as well as the affective problems.

E-mail: RichardSide@eckersley.co.uk

2.7 The benefits and limitations of consciousness-raising training in L2 writing

Catherine Matsuo *Fukuoka University, Japan*

Aim

This study aimed to compare the effects on writing performance of an externalized, i.e. separate, programme of consciousness-raising training about L2 writing tasks with a course where the methodology elicited strategy-use and learners asked questions about tasks, but there was no explicit, systematic training.

The study

The subjects were two small groups (11 and 13 students) of Japanese university English majors with substantial knowledge of formal grammar, but little experience of writing beyond sentence-level. For nine months, I taught both groups (90 minutes, weekly) with a genre-based process approach, i.e. a methodology innovation. The trained group received explicit training based on Wenden's (1995) task knowledge; the untrained group received only what consciousness-raising occurred through tasks themselves and a 'question/comment/answer' session whose content they determined. (These lasted the same amount of time as the 'trained' group's training sessions.) Pre-treatment, both groups wrote a timed essay (50 minutes, no dictionary); they were then told that they would write the same essay again the following week under the same conditions, and could do whatever they wished in preparation. This procedure was repeated nine months later with the same essay topic (long enough to reduce the practice effect). i.e. students wrote two drafts both pre- and post-treatment. Following each second draft, students reported the strategies they had used from a questionnaire selection. (Three raters – scores correlated – marked the second drafts, using the ESL Composition Profile.)

Results

The pre-treatment timed essay second draft scores revealed that the groups had started out statistically different: the trained group scored higher. However, both groups reported using the same number of strategies. Post-treatment, both groups' writing had improved significantly, and the groups' scores were statistically similar: the untrained group had 'caught up'. Both groups' reported use of strategies increased, but the trained group reported (1) using more strategies on average than the untrained group, and (2) to a greater extent than the untrained group using 'higher level' strategies of considering genre and reader, i.e. characteristics of more expert writers. Most remarkable were regression analysis findings: pre-treatment, there was no strong relationship for either group between the number of strategies reported used and essay scores. Post-treatment, while there was still no relationship between reported strategy use for the untrained group, the number of strategies reported used by the trained group related strongly to their scores, i.e. the trained group was using more strategies and managing them efficiently.

Conclusion

The groups were very small and not similar, pre-treatment, so no absolute conclusions can be drawn. However, this study suggests that learners with little experience of creating extended discourse benefit from an externalized programme because it allows them to focus clearly and systematically on various task dimensions. Also, this seems to promote faster proceduralization, better understanding of goals (Bereiter and Scardamalia 1987) and effective strategy management. One drawback is that focusing on strategies seems to take time away from writing, and although both groups improved, the trained group did not retain their 'lead' over the untrained group in terms of writing performance, post-treatment.

E-mail: cath@fukuoka-u.ac.jp

2.8 Preventing the basketball effect: Incorporating student revision in the writing process

Karlheinz Ribisch and Lisa Nazarenko *Vienna University, Austria*

What we have, slightly ironically, dubbed the 'basketball effect' is the not uncommon reaction of learners who see no point in dealing with their homework once they get it back from the teacher and feel there is no way in which they can learn from their mistakes. Instead, they hardly look at the homework sheet the teacher has just returned to them, crumple it up and, skilfully, in the fashion of a top basketball player, toss it into the wastepaper basket.

It was the aim of our workshop to show how, by having learners write two drafts of each writing assignment, we try to make text-writing more meaningful for the learner, while by the same token, the corrections which the teacher makes become much more relevant. We also feel that the requirement to revise their texts increases learners' independence in developing their own style and their ability to critique their own writing.

The learners see that improvement is possible. They are given a second chance and the fact that, at least in our experience, the second version is always better than the first draft, raises learners' self-confidence and motivation. The second version gives learners the idea that what they have produced is close, or at least closer to what could be called a 'finished product', which results in a feeling that they have actually achieved something. They can see how they are making progress.

In addition, a strong sense of teacher–learner co-operation develops. Once students have got used to this system, they begin to see the teacher's corrections of the first draft as helpful indications as to what needs to be changed and where improvement is possible. The teachers, on the other hand, gain much greater job satisfaction from the fact that their efforts and the time they have spent correcting are not wasted. Correcting is also less monotonous, as the 'same old mistakes' appear less frequently. On the whole, the teacher gets the impression that s/he is really making a difference.

Making the writing of a second version of a text a requirement has also meant a considerable change in the way in which we correct texts. Most importantly, this system allows us to reduce the number of instances where we directly tell the learner, 'This is what you should have written.' Instead, our margin notes contain more indirect feedback, suggestions, questions, etc. As a result, learners need to look things up in dictionaries, for example, and thus the responsibility for the correction is, at least to a certain extent, shifted from the teacher to the learner.

In the workshop, we showed that there are various ways to correct a text and give feedback. But the point was also made that though teachers will tend to use different approaches and different correction symbols, what really counts is fine-tuning and adapting your system to the needs of the learners.

E-mail: kh.ribisch@vienna.at
lisa.nazarenko@aon.at

2.9 When a day is all you have

Edwina S Carreon *Ohio State University, USA*

It is a common sight: ESL/EFL writing teachers grading papers alone in their offices. One consequence is often a lack of common assessment standards for marking student work. This presentation is a result of my experience assisting the English Language Education Department (ELED) at De La Salle University in the Philippines in developing writing assessment guidelines or grading rubrics for use in their undergraduate writing courses. Designing the training workshop was challenging for a number of reasons:

1 No ready-made set of grading guidelines has proved satisfactory so far, so rubrics had to be 'tailor-made'.
2 Course co-ordinators were to be involved in development of the guidelines or rubrics and, consequently, some foundation in writing assessment was a parallel objective.
3 We had only one day (five hours) to accomplish both objectives.

Session topics

The uses of writing assessment, writing scales and bands, and reader training

Course co-ordinators ranked this the most useful topic to them because it convinced them of the need for common standards and established a shared discourse for later discussions on assessment.

A review of scoring approaches
In particular, holistic, primary trait and analytic scoring based on Wolcott and Legg (1998).

Drafting ELED grading rubrics
We focused on one required course taught by all teachers. To encourage reflection on their own assessment standards, participants analyzed course objectives stated in the course syllabus and compared them with the explicit and implicit requirements of one essay examination prompt recently used on the course. Using shared ideas and discourse from this discussion, the participants then assigned grades ranging from 4 (best) to 1 (poor) to a set of four pre-selected 'anchor' papers chosen from actual student essays. Group discussion followed, in which participants compared their grade assignments. This activity and a second set of 'anchor' papers followed by discussion became the basis for the initial draft set of rubrics.

Calibration sessions
To test the rubrics and participants' interpretations of them, additional sets of 'anchor' papers based on new topics were given.

Strategies used

Extend time
Given the time constraints, I conducted an informal needs analysis weeks before actually arriving in Manila. Also, by gathering materials from the department days in advance, I was able to use materials that were familiar and relevant to the participants. Finally, I encouraged the participants to refine the instrument on their own, staying in touch with the department head during the process.

Use technology
I took advantage of available high and low technology: e-mail and telephone to plan the programme; a courier service to send and receive materials; a computer for my PowerPoint presentation; an electronic whiteboard to facilitate note-taking; a photocopier to make multiple copies of whiteboard notes; a video camera to film important segments for later review and training of other faculty, and e-mail to send and return session feedback questionnaires.

Conclusion

The training session was successful as a result of the strategies used, the participants' willingness to communicate, and administrative support. Despite the time constraint, the training was also effective in raising teachers' awareness of their varied assessment practices, the need for a collaborative understanding of writing standards, and the department's ability to take ownership of the assessment standards used to evaluate their student papers.

E-mail: carreon.1@osu.edu

2.10 EST activities for mixed-ability groups

Yuliya Siderova *Naval Academy, Bulgaria*

English for Science and Technology lessons may be considered rather dry and mainly comprised of reading and translation tasks, which unfortunately very often turns out to be the case. The situation becomes even more challenging in mixed-level groups where learners have different expectations about their EST classes.

At the beginning of the English for Electronics course at the Naval Academy in Varna two basic groups of trainees are usually formed. One of them (G1) consists of trainees who are not very good at English, but are good at electronics. They feel confident in their professional knowledge, and their motivation for studying EST exists from the very beginning. The other group (G2) consists of trainees who are very good at English, but not at electronics, and who are quite disappointed by the matter-of-fact style of technical English. What is the ESP teacher supposed to do in such a situation?

Since our trainees will need most of all to develop their reading skills, reading tasks are extremely important. The type of task usually depends on what is suggested by the selected text. Speaking skills are not the goal of our ESP training, but they are a very efficient means of achieving that goal. For G2, speaking tasks provide opportunities to practise their language competence, and they give G1 the feeling they are making real progress because, since they are familiar with and interested in the subject matter, it is easier for them to overcome their anxiety and lack of confidence. The usual speaking practice is discussion on a topic, but a really good discussion is usually impossible in the early ESP classes because of the insufficient vocabulary of G1, and insufficient knowledge of the subject matter of G2.

The writing task we use most commonly is describing a figure (usually an electronic circuit). When we start writing circuit descriptions, the first problem we encounter is that usually only G1 trainees can read electronic circuits. In terms of language competence, this is not a problem – in fact it is an advantage, since the trainees can express uncertainty by using modal verbs, conditional sentences, etc. However, what usually happens with a circuit description task is that a G1 trainee explains the operation of the circuit in Bulgarian, and then everybody starts writing. That gave me the idea of using circuit description as a speaking task even in earlier ESP classes – a G1 trainee tries to explain the operation of the circuit to a G2 trainee – the former has a great deal of professional information which he tries to express through his limited amount of English, and the second one uses all his language competence to get the professional information he lacks.

The purpose of this rather artificial classification of the EST trainees is to try to solve some of the problems which arise in a mixed-ability ESP group, and even turn some of the disadvantages of such a situation into advantages by stimulating co-operation and competition.

E-mail: siderova@yahoo.com

2.11 Building the foundation: The challenge of university preparation

Theresa McKinven *Durham University, England*

The challenges faced by many university language centres in the UK are changing. In the past, much university English language teaching focused on enabling post-graduate students, with knowledge of their subjects, to transfer existing knowledge and skills to English. The growth of foundation courses for pre-undergraduate overseas students has meant that many universities have had to reconsider their provision for these students. Many of these students arrive with limited English, little knowledge of their degree subject, and little awareness of accepted academic standards of behaviour, but at the same time with extremely high expectations. They often encounter difficulties, as a result of their youth and immaturity, and though motivated, may lack appropriate direction.

With such students there can often be a major conflict of expectation. The centre and teachers may expect to continue to use the approaches and programmes that have proved successful in the past. The students may expect more traditional teacher–student roles, and equate 'grammar' with language teaching, being in class with learning. They may spend a lot of time studying, but that study may be based on previous study patterns and expectations, memorising grammar rules, or reproducing knowledge rather than analysing or challenging it.

One of the major challenges facing those studying and teaching on preparatory courses is maintaining motivation over a long period of time. Many courses last nine months or longer, and it can be difficult for students to perceive the progress they have made. Students may become impatient with what they believe to be slow progress. This can lead them to blame the teachers, the programme, the teaching methods, the centre. It can be very difficult at these times for the course tutors to retain confidence in the programme.

At Durham, we faced these challenges and more when the small preparatory programme was expanded by the arrival of a group of young middle-eastern students, intending to study law. Over the last two years, we have developed strategies to address the needs of these students. Staffing is key – teachers have been employed from outside the area, to meet the need for greater experience and qualifications, and specialism in legal English. The course is university accredited, so interim goals can be set and students can obtain university certificates. One module on the programme, entitled 'Language in the Community', provides the students with the opportunity to study relevant aspects of British life. Every effort has been made to ensure that this module did not become the study of 'British culture', but instead would be a critical exploration by the students and teacher, a highly experienced social studies teacher, of present day multi-cultural Britain.

There is no doubt that this programme has been a positive development for the centre, and for the students. In their second year with us, they have shown greater intellectual maturity, and have recently taken their first law exam. From comments made by the audience, it was apparent that these issues are shared by many institutions concerned with preparing young students for university study.

E-mail: Theresa.McKinven@durham.ac.uk

2.12 IELTS preparation: Views of teachers and students

Anthony Green *University of Surrey at Roehampton, England*

This presentation reported the attitudes of groups of teachers and learners in the UK towards IELTS preparation.

Subjects and methods

Interview: five teachers with both IELTS preparation and other English for Academic Purposes (EAP) teaching experience.

Survey: 30 students, mixed nationalities on three courses: each involving a different model of IELTS preparation.

Teachers' views

Teachers drew a clear distinction between the content of IELTS and EAP classes. They reported a range of test preparation practices, but saw IELTS classes as being primarily directed at success in the test (with student pressure on the teachers to conform to this aim) at the expense of broader EAP skills. Narrow IELTS test preparation was seen to boost students' scores on the test, although score gains might not be matched by more general improvements in ability. Success at IELTS was not necessarily felt to be indicative of readiness for university study in Britain. Teachers disagreed on which activities were most appropriate to IELTS preparation – for example, some included grammar correction in their classes, others text summaries. However, there was a common core of distinctive preparation activities including:

- test-taking strategies – e.g. rehearsing interview technique
- teaching how to describe graphs and trends

Test-taking practice

On the other hand, some activities, including the following, were seen as typifying EAP, but were under-represented in IELTS preparation:

- process writing (planning, drafting, revising)
- lengthy essay writing
- teaching note-taking/note-making skills
- individual project work
- referencing, quoting and synthesising sources

These differences were generally supported by the 12 IATEFL delegates with IELTS experience, who completed a survey based on the teacher responses. Overall, IELTS preparation activities were seen as useful in university preparation, but involving a narrower focus than desirable.

Students' views

Students identified tasks they felt would contribute most to success at IELTS. Generally, these reflected test content (writing short essays, reading and answering short-answer questions). On the other hand, the students rated grammar exercises the third most helpful activity for passing the test. This seemed surprising, as IELTS includes no grammar sub-test. The importance of grammar for students may reflect its role in the IELTS Writing and Speaking scoring criteria, or a persistent belief in the importance of grammatical knowledge in language learning. Popular EAP tasks such as independent projects, oral presentations and lengthy essays were regarded as least useful for passing IELTS. Generally, students saw hard work as the best guarantor of success, and felt they were working harder than usual in pursuit of a passing grade (although the amount of independent study done outside class apparently varied considerably: between 0 and 40 hours per week).

Individuals clearly have idiosyncratic strategies for meeting test demands, but share the view that test preparation focuses narrowly on test content at the expense of broader skills. If this is so, it seems possible that students arriving at university with acceptable IELTS scores may not have adequate preparation in EAP to meet the demands of their studies.

E-mail: a.b.green@btinternet.com

2.13 A way with classical art

Monika Seidl *Vienna University, Austria*

Visuals work as stimulating learning resources because they are 'texts where students provide the words'. In my presentation, I argued that classical art, and specifically representational paintings, work well with students at all levels. In contrast to photographs, which are often used as stimuli, classical art is more detached from my students' way of life and everyday experience, and therefore provides a context for language learning which is more 'open'. I developed the idea of 'openness' further and came up with two types of 'open' paintings, both of which I have found suitable for language learning purposes. Type one, which I labelled 'Openness outside', refers to paintings where the people depicted point towards something outside the frame, something invisible, or partially hidden, thereby leaving a gap which students find it stimulating to fill. (Examples include Velázquez, *Las Meninas*, 1657, Manet, *Le Balcon*, 1868, or *Gare Saint-Lazare*, 1873.) 'Openness within', the second type of 'openness', refers to paintings whose mood is very evocative because of a close link between the people depicted and a very telling setting. Students find it easy to capture what might be going on 'inside' the heads of those people when they work with this second type of painting. (Examples include paintings by Edward Hopper such as *Cape Cod Evening*, 1939, or Caspar David Friedrich's *Chalk Cliffs on Rügen*, 1818.)

The activities presented ranged from some suitable for beginners to others for very advanced learners of English taking part in a literature programme. Beginners can use the paintings as stimuli for simple oral exercises, which involve questions and answers about the people depicted. Intermediate learners use the pictures to practise the speaking module that is part of many official language exams. On an advanced writing course I use the paintings for point-of-view sketches. This latter activity was further developed to put across theoretical approaches to literature, such as feminism.

I use the following generic assignment with advanced learners of English:

- *Look at the picture and interpret what is happening in any way you like. Write at least two accounts of the scene, but before doing so, decide which points of view you wish to adopt.*
- *Who are the two narrators? Are they from outside or inside the painting? Are they from the centre or the fringe?*
- *Remember that you can write from several positions: from an external position, which is detached and without insight; from an internal position, which sees only what one character sees; or from an all-seeing, all-knowing position.*
- *Decide on the personalities of your narrators (e.g. hesitant, confident, boastful, ashamed...), and the tone they adopt (e.g. amused, detached, outraged, ironic, arrogant, unpleasant...)*
- *If your narrators are human, also think of a profession for them, which could then appear through the way that they speak, the similes used, the comments made (e.g. sports-person, teacher, lorry-driver, butcher, psychiatrist, politician...).*

Now relate the scene in the picture, choosing at least two points of view. You can choose to relate a very brief scene (the few minutes before or after the scene depicted) or a longer story, including what happened further back in the past and what happens afterwards.

After writing your accounts, comment briefly on the effects you wanted to achieve, and briefly describe the two narrators you have chosen.

E-mail: monika.seidl@univie.ac.at

2.14 All the world's a stage: Shakespeare for EFL students

Robert Hill *University of Verona, Italy*

The following task-types have proved stimulating with EFL students approaching Shakespeare:

Minimal response questions

When students are asked for interpretations, their answers are often hesitant: unsurprising if they have little critical confidence – 'Nothing will come of nothing', as King Lear says to Cordelia. Additionally, students' production generally lags behind their reading skills, which also blocks responses. Useful tools for encouraging interpretation are activity types from EFL methodology – multiple choice, true/false, matching, sequencing, gap-filling, ranking – which offer a 'menu' of interpretations to choose from and initially require minimal production for responses. But once choices have been made, students will defend and justify them, and this is where real interpretation begins. Students can modify their choices to bring them closer to their own interpretation, or create their own interpretation, based on the 'menu' presented to them. Multiple choice can be based on one line, a scene, an act, a complete play, or even all of Shakespeare!

Charts relating a play or a character to other texts or characters

This technique encourages a diachronic/comparative approach to Shakespeare, and identifies both Shakespeare's timelessness and his originality. Texts for comparison can be dramatic or not (e.g. novels, poems, films, etc.), fictional or not (from real life, newspaper articles, etc.): the other characters can be fictional or not. Just one example must serve. On the left-hand side of a chart students find the key elements of *Romeo and Juliet*:

a) The story ends with the death of one or both of the lovers.
b) One or both of the lovers falls in love at first sight, or in a very short time.
c) Their love is 'impossible': it must be kept secret.
d) The lovers are very young and good-looking.
e) The lovers have a very short period of happiness before catastrophe strikes.
f) One of the lovers has had a previous, unsatisfactory experience of love.
g) The woman declares her love first.
h) Most of the lovers' meetings take place by night.

On the right-hand side students write in any love story they choose – classic or recent, fictional or real – and decide whether it conforms to these elements or not. With this procedure it becomes clear why *Titanic* was so successful. It follows closely the plot of *Romeo and Juliet*: even the span of the love affair is the same – three days! Shakespeare's originality also emerges – it is very rare in fiction for a woman to dare to declare her love first.

Suggesting film versions

Students are familiar with film conventions, and have had exposure to the advantages that film has over staging: tracking and panning to direct focus of attention; cutting (effective for moving rapidly in place and time to bring out situational irony); zoom and close-ups to show nuances of expression difficult to show on stage; voiceover (for irony of situation, or to communicate deeper or more tentative thoughts in soliloquies); limitless possibilities for lighting effects and soundtrack.

Aware of these opportunities, students can explore problem-solving activities such as: How do Romeo and Juliet fall in love at first sight at a masked ball? How can Macbeth's castle be presented? (Duncan and Banquo find it pleasant on arrival, yet it *must* be menacing.) Shakespeare's major plays have been filmed several times, so students' suggestions can be compared with more than one film solution.

E-mail: robhill@tin.it

2.15 Colour your lesson with films: A film workshop

Dr Ali Nihat Eken *Bilkent University, Turkey*

Feature films can be a valuable tool for promoting critical thinking skills, enhancing students' listening, speaking, reading and writing skills, and increasing their appreciation of arts and artists. They can help students to think along various dimensions and thus gain control over media texts instead of simply accepting them superficially. They can also open doors to various disciplines, e.g. cultural studies, media studies and film studies, which can bring diversity into language classrooms.

In order to create a context for my students to practise their English and develop their critical thinking skills, I designed a 14-week undergraduate course called Media Studies. In the first ten weeks of the course, I focused on deconstruction and analysis of various media texts such as commercials, films, television and radio programmes. In the last four weeks of the course, I divided my students into four groups and asked them to prepare and carry out a film workshop where they analyzed the film *You've Got Mail*. I assigned each group an aspect of the film (literary aspects, dramatic aspects, cinematic aspects, language work), and provided each group with a sample framework they could use while analyzing the film. I also asked them to create activities or tasks to use in their workshop. The preparation and the workshop itself took place over four weeks.

At the end of the workshop I conducted group interviews to see how studying films had contributed to my students' learning. I made some notes during the interviews and later analyzed these in four categories that seemed to emerge from the data:

- **critical thinking skills**: The workshop helped students become active viewers through gaining awareness of how films are constructed, how pieces or details make up a whole, and how they can be deconstructed for a richer analysis. Questioning, examining aspects of a film and applying film theories enhanced students' critical thinking skills.
- **psychological effects**: The workshop increased students' confidence in speaking in front of an audience. After completing the workshop, they felt satisfied that they could be very creative. Students also believed that they had gained a measure of intellectual maturity in their appreciation of the arts.
- **effects of studying films on real-life situations**: After practising the analysis of films, students started to look at life more critically. A close analysis of characters, events and values in films helped them to do the same thing in real life.
- **language skills**: The film workshop provided students with a rich context through which they could practise their English by listening, speaking, reading and writing. They also learned some new vocabulary.

The media studies course and the film workshop indicate that films can be very valuable tools in the English language classroom. An important point to keep in mind, however, is that films should be viewed as subject matter in their own right and be used with a principled approach, aiming to improve students' abilities, not just in language but also in critical and creative thinking.

E-mail: eken@bilkent.edu.tr

2.16 Plenary: Teachers versus television: A short history of visual media in ELT

Susan Stempleski and Barry Tomalin

The title of this talk was inspired by Michael Medved's *Hollywood vs. America*. In that provocative book, Medved argues that the values of Hollywood movies are polluting

American values. Our adaptation of his title does something different. It highlights the use of visual media in ELT and the fact that – unlike the portable audio cassette recorder that English teachers have taken to their hearts – visually-based technologies such as video and multimedia have not become part of everybody's language lesson, ELT curriculum or classroom methodology. We try to explain why that has happened and ask the question, 'Has the time of visual media in ELT finally come?'

In the process, we look at the use of the video and television, both in the classroom and for self-study. We look at where we have been and where we are now, and point out some trends for the future, along with some key issues facing teachers who wish to make more of visual technology in their teaching.

Our central thesis is that television and video are unique language learning delivery systems that have not been fully embraced by teachers. What we aim to do here is to explore why this has happened and what the pedagogical objections have been, and show how producers of visual media in the twenty-first century are learning some of the lessons textbook writers absorbed in the 1980s and 1990s.

Key issues

Visual-based technology is multi-faceted. It encompasses television, video and multimedia delivery systems. Our examination of the ELT media that have been produced using these visual technologies focuses on four key issues: *production* (Who produced it? What were the production approaches? How did they reflect or contribute to ELT methodology?), *technology* (How did the technology develop? What was the impact on materials? How did it affect the use of visual materials in ELT?), *methodology* (How were teachers and learners expected to use material?), and *audience* (For what learners was the material produced?). Our major observations under these headings include the following:

Production: Production considerations and expense determine to a great extent how much visual media are made available to language teachers and learners. Because of the great expense involved in producing high-quality video and television material, government has played an important role in financing and broadcasting such visual media for ELT.

Technology: The massive advances in technology in the last forty years have made the video player, the DVD player and the multimedia computer the most common technologies for entertainment and learning available in the more advanced economies. However, while these technologies are widely used at home, they are much more rarely used in classrooms.

Methodology: New and adapted methodologies have evolved, which have been exploited by the new technologies in ELT. The drivers in this case have been the development of the functional–notional approach to language learning and teaching developed by Wilkins and others in the 1960s, which was the basis of the communicative method in English language teaching in the 1970s and 1980s, and the production of the Threshold and Waystage specifications for language learning in 1973, which provided the basis for many course designs for TV and video English courses.

Audience: There are different audiences for ELT video and television. To cite just a few examples, these media can be used for training students in the classroom, for training individual learners at home, for presenting demonstration lessons to teachers, or for delivering examination material. Each of these environments places different demands on the visual media employed.

We begin our history with a flashback and a look at a very early ELT television series for absolute beginners.

The early stages: *Walter and Connie*

The first Europe-wide success in ELT on television made its début in 1962. It was the *Walter and Connie* series produced by the BBC in financial collaboration with the British Council. The series was produced in black and white on 16-millimetre film and projected onto a screen or shown on television. In the series, Walter and Connie, a young married couple, found themselves in a number of 'typically British' situations. The language points being taught in each episode were highlighted in on-screen captions accompanied by a certain amount of on-screen drilling, with Connie eliciting the unseen student response. This was direct teaching of the audience with dramatic situations (in the form of situation comedies) as the vehicle for presenting new language. The approach was structural/situational, and the methodology followed a simple three-step formula: (1) preparation for viewing, (2) watch and (3) follow-up, with comprehension questions, script study and simple book-based exercises. This basic methodological formula for using TV and film in ELT prevailed throughout the 1960s. The study package consisted of a film and an accompanying self-study book. This multiple-media package set a model that would last for forty years.

The great value of *Walter and Connie* was that for learners across Europe it brought the outside world into the classroom and increased students' motivation to learn. The idea of using the world outside the classroom to engage, involve and motivate learners has remained a standard principle of television- and video-based learning.

Video as a classroom resource: *The Bellcrest Story*

In 1973, just a little more than a decade after the debut of *Walter and Connie*, the BBC, working in cooperation with the British Council and Oxford University Press, released *The Bellcrest Story*. This full-colour series focused on business English for advanced learners and was a big and exciting move from the black and white of *Walter and Connie*. It broke new ground in a number of other ways, too. It had a gripping and continuing storyline and was produced and directed as a full broadcast-quality TV drama. *The Bellcrest Story* not only marked the breakthrough into more natural television, it also highlighted a major methodological advance by introducing the idea of television and film as a classroom resource. In contrast to the very obvious language lessons embedded in the televised adventures of *Walter and Connie*, the episodes of *The Bellcrest Story* contained no explicit teaching. Instead, they immersed viewer-learners in a realistically acted drama with naturally spoken dialogue that employed language appropriate to the students' business needs. It was the other elements in the learning package – namely, the course book and the audiocassettes – that provided learners and teachers with explicit language teaching material.

While *The Bellcrest Story* introduced the idea of video and film as a classroom resource, the series presented the same problems as *Walter and Connie* in terms of classroom exploitation, that is, how could teachers actually use the film or television material in class? In the video-rich universe of today, it's important to remember that *The Bellcrest Story* was not a video series. It was distributed on 16-millimetre film, and this made all the difference as to how it could be used. As anyone who has ever used 16-millimetre film in the classroom knows, when using a film projector, you cannot freeze the picture to study a particular frame, nor can you rewind and replay a particular segment very easily. And you certainly can't fast forward to a particular film frame. What this meant was that teachers using *The Bellcrest Story* followed the same three-step methodology (preparation, watch, follow-up) that they had used with *Walter and Connie.*

Putting teaching with video on the map: *Follow Me*

The breakthrough in television and video ELT worldwide came through the development of the videocassette recorder and compact VHS PAL and NTSC videocassettes, together with the production of the most successful ELT television series ever developed. This was *Follow Me*, a 60-unit course based on the Council of Europe Waystage and Threshold Level English specifications and following a functional-notional course design developed by Louis Alexander. The *Follow Me* programmes had a modular structure. Each fifteen-minute programme combined a developing comedy (sitcom) fronted by that most English of actors, Francis Matthews, with documentary, drama and animation elements combined with language summaries through on-screen captions. This modular approach also set a pattern for other language-teaching television programmes that followed. Initially produced for an adult audience in Germany who were training for the German Adult Education Certificate, *Follow Me* was eventually watched by hundreds of millions of people in over 70 countries.

Launched in 1979, the *Follow Me* series was the first move away from fairly straightforward structural-situational teaching into a more functional approach. Its other great value was its modular structure. Instead of viewers watching a complete episode right through as they had done with *The Bellcrest Story*, they could now watch short, self-contained bits, which could be taken out of sequence and used individually in a classroom. At the same time the VHS cassette (PAL or NTSC format) provided, at a price, a technology the teacher could access. Suddenly video became a real possibility in the classroom.

Follow Me was supported by both audiocassettes and books, and a distance education support programme was developed in Germany through the German adult education centres (*Volkshochschulen*). The appearance of *Follow Me* marked the development, already presaged by *The Bellcrest Story,* of what we now call 'multiple media courses'. We used to call them '*multimedia* courses', but, as everyone knows, that term has since been hijacked by producers and distributors of digital media. So *multiple* media would be television, video, radio, audio, and books – all working together – to teach a language. And the most widespread example of that was in *Follow Me.*

At the time that *Follow Me* appeared, publishing companies such as Nelson Filmscan had also begun developing video courses for ESP and general English in the classroom. A feature of these courses was the incorporation of communicative methods in teaching English with video. This involved the development of information-gap type activities where the students had to communicate with each other to solve problems set up by the video and accompanying course book. Leading writers and publishers – such as Peter and Karen Viney for Oxford University Press and Ingrid Freebairn and Brian Abbs for Longman – began developing video-based dramas to accompany their best-selling coursebooks, *Grapevine* and *Strategies*. One of the most successful developments in this genre was Robert O'Neill's extraordinary *The Lost Secret* for the BBC, in which he successfully transferred the 'thriller' concept of his seminal 'The Man Who Escaped' in *Kernel Lessons Intermediate* from print to video.

Teacher training for video

The introduction of the modular approach into ELT video allowed more opportunities for using videocassettes in the classroom, and in more flexible ways. However, these opportunities and ways were not immediately apparent to most teachers who, like almost everyone else who viewed television, were used to simply *watching* television and not doing anything with it other than letting the full programme run through. As a response to the need to provide teachers with training in the use of ELT video, Joe Hambrook brought together a small group of people at the 1987 IATEFL International Conference in Westende, Belgium, and created what at that time was known as the IATEFL Video SIG (Special Interest Group), and which has since been re-christened the IATEFL Media SIG.

Inspired by the development of the IATEFL Video SIG, a short while later a group of video-users at the 1987 TESOL Convention, in Miami, Florida came together and called for the development of a special interest group within TESOL that would serve as an additional international network for the sharing of video experience and expertise. From the late 1980s through the 1990s, the IATEFL Video SIG and the TESOL Video IS (Interest Section) worked together closely and both got involved in teacher training. Their publications – *TESOL Video News* and *Small Screen* – stressed two stages of training: (1) how to use the hardware (video equipment), and (2) how to exploit the software (videos). In other words, they initially trained teachers to use the video equipment, and this initial stage then evolved into a methodology for exploiting the videos themselves.

Video-based methodology

The methodology promoted by the IATEFL Video SIG and the TESOL Video IS integrated communicative language teaching (CLT) techniques with the capabilities of video technology. It was a methodology characterized by teaching activities in which teachers created the information-gap type activities characteristic of CLT by manipulating the video equipment (e.g. 'silent viewing' activities in which students view the pictures on the video monitor but do not hear the soundtrack) or the audience (e.g. 'split viewing' activities in which some of the students were allowed to see the video and hear the soundtrack, while others only got to hear the soundtrack).

Teachers' resistance to video

In spite of the developments in production approaches, technology and methodology, it was apparent that although teachers had adopted the portable audiocassette recorder, they were much more resistant to the use of video in the classroom. There were a number of reasons for this. One was the video equipment itself. It was expensive but not portable. Security and storage were big problems and not very easily overcome. As it was, teachers who wanted to incorporate video into their lessons had to book rooms, find keys, and also find the necessary space and time, as well as access to equipment, in order to cue the videos and prepare video-based lessons.

In addition to issues related to security and storage, there was the problem of the hostile nature of the equipment itself. There were all those cables and buttons to deal with. At their very best, early videocassette players were a long way from being 'teacher-friendly'. Counters varied from machine to machine. Different video players might or might not have facilities such as pause or freeze-frame buttons. Rewind facilities broke down very quickly. And smoothly operating the 'memory' function was not something most teachers, or anyone else for that matter, would immediately intuit. Had combined television and video players been available in the 1970s, the use of video in ELT might have been different and much more widespread.

A third reason for teachers' resistance to video was related to the ELT syllabus. Many teachers found it difficult enough to find time to get through the assigned coursebooks, so they felt there was no time to incorporate supplementary video material into the teaching programme. This put publishers in a paradoxical situation in which they had to publish videos to accompany courses that would be used by only a minority of teachers.

A fourth reason for teachers' resistance was the perception by students and teachers of television and video as devices for relaxation. As a result, teachers tended to limit their use of video to end-of-term projects or Friday afternoon 'video shows', rather than use it in ways that acknowledged and exploited its full linguistic and methodological potential.

A final reason for teachers' resistance to video has to do with the universal nature of the content of ELT video. Because of the expense involved in producing ELT television and video, the products that were produced were designed for as wide an audience as possible. Thus, at a time when textbooks began to adapt to national audiences and regional realities, television and video remained general resources reflecting the producers' and writers' views of the life and language of the target culture.

Video for teacher training

An important sub-development of the use of video in ELT has been its importance in teacher training and development. By and large, producers such as the British Council or the BBC have adopted one of two approaches: an 'observational' approach or a 'best practice' approach. In the 'observational' approach adopted by Cambridge University Press and the British Council, video is used to present a complete lesson from beginning to end. This video is then used as a basis for group observation, analysis and discussion.

In the 'best practice' approach, instructional videos feature excerpts showing 'best practice' techniques from demonstration lessons. A leading example of this is the *Teaching Observed* series produced in the 1970s by the BBC in collaboration with the British

Council. This series of twelve 25-minute teacher-training films was shot in classrooms in Ghana, Botswana, Sri Lanka and Singapore.

Another example of the 'best practice' approach, and one which is of particular interest here, is *Video in the English Class*, a 30-minute video produced by the BBC in 1990. This teacher training video featured ten short excerpts from video-based lessons employing key techniques for successful teaching with video. The video highlighted information gap techniques such as 'silent viewing', 'sound only' and 'split viewing' and reinforced the idea of using video to stimulate language use by the students, rather than simply as a tool for pre-teaching and reinforcing target language vocabulary and structural patterns.

The American dimension

The year 1991 witnessed the appearance of *Family Album USA*, published by Prentice Hall Regents in the USA in cooperation with the United States Information Agency. This project marked the beginnings of US government investment in ELT video. The 26-episode English-by-broadcast programme was designed as both an intermediate level ELT television series and a video-based classroom course. The television programme, which has been broadcast in over 50 countries, tells the story of the Stewart family, a 'typical' upper middle-class American family. The action is presented in a series of 30-minute soap opera episodes, each of which is divided into three acts. Between the acts, short music and animation segments provide a break from the realistic approach of the drama and offer a livelier, more explicit presentation of the language items used in the acts.

In 1998, another American publisher, McGraw-Hill, working together with WGBH Boston, a public television station, produced a groundbreaking ELT television series called *Connect with English*. Aimed at high-beginner through intermediate levels, the series, comprised of forty-eight 15-minute episodes, tells the story of Rebecca Casey, an aspiring young singer, on a journey across America from her hometown of Boston, Massachusetts to San Francisco, California.

The series is notable for a number of reasons. One is its geographical scope. Filmed on a wide range of locations across the whole of the US, *Connect with English* takes a realistic look at both the geographical variety and the ethnic diversity that is characteristic of the US. A second notable feature is the series' combination of scripted and unscripted language. The dramatic episodes of the soap opera are followed by talk show sequences in which adult English language learners comment on and discuss the action of the episodes in relation to their own lives. Another distinctive feature of the series is its use of non native speakers as an integral part of the programme, thus exposing viewers to a variety of non-native accents at the same time as providing them with successful models of English language learners.

Video for children

Video has always been perceived as a major way of motivating children to learn, and over the history of ELT video there have been a number of series aimed specifically at pre-school and primary school age learners. In the year 2000, Children's Television Workshop, the producers of *Sesame Street*, introduced *Sesame English*, a multiple-media initiative for three- to eleven-year-old children around the world. The backbone of the *Sesame English* project is a 15-minute, 52-episode television series produced by Sesame Workshop in association with Berlitz Languages. The programme features Tingo, a new Muppet character created by the Jim Henson Company, along with many familiar *Sesame Street* characters. Tingo speaks every language under the sun, including the native language of his viewing audience wherever in the world he travels. The shows use comedy, physical action and music to introduce basic English to young viewers. Each episode follows a comic story line embedded in a magazine format featuring Sesame Street's Muppet animation and live-action inserts.

An adjunct and distinguishing feature of the *Sesame English* series is the *Sesame English Variety Show*, a locally produced series designed to complement *Sesame English*. The show, currently being broadcast in Shanghai and scheduled to début in Japan in the near future, uses local hosts and children to re-invent the *Sesame English* curriculum through games, songs and activities, in which local children play a very active role. Like *Connect with English, Sesame English* is an example of a developing trend toward using non-native speakers as language models.

Current trends

So in the present day, what are the key trends in the visual media? We have identified four, three of which are exhibited by *Crossroads Café*, a lively 26-episode television and video series centering on six characters and Crossroads Café, a neighbourhood restaurant. These four trends are:

1 Multiple investment

The *Crossroads Café* series represents an unprecedented collaboration in the history of ELT video. The series was developed in the US in 1996 through a partnership between the State Education Agencies of four states (California, Florida, Illinois and New York), INTELECOM Intelligent Telecommunications (a California-based consortium of colleges and universities), the US Immigration and Naturalization Service, Heinle & Heinle Publishers, the PBS Adult Learning service, and the United States Information Agency. Because of the cost of video production, and the growing demand for more sophisticated and wide-ranging products, it seems safe to say that the pattern of multiple investment will remain with us in the foreseeable future.

2 Learners as leads

The relationship to the audience has developed to the point where now the lead characters and language models are second language learners. The *Crossroads Café* focuses on six main characters, and four of them are non-native speakers of English!

3 Similarity to mainstream television

The third trend is the obscuring of the barrier between ELT production values and the production values of mainstream television. *Crossroads Café* is in the form of what its producers refer to as a 'dramedy' – a blending of drama and comedy. Like regular (i.e. non-ELT) television situation comedies, the series has a laugh track (recorded laughter added to the soundtrack of the video), and each half-hour episode is designed to fit into a regular 30-minute television time slot. Another feature that marks its similarity to mainstream television is its focus on diverse ethnicities and real-world scenarios.

4 Digital media

Finally, we move from multiple media – television, video, radio, audio, and print for self-study – to digital media. The current trend is to develop visual ELT material that can be adapted to any format, now or in the future. An example of this is *Goal,* a new BBC teenage series that combines ELT with sophisticated presentation – exactly as *The Bellcrest Story* did in the early seventies! The series is in the form of a multimedia program in digital format that can be developed as television broadcast, video, DVD, multimedia, or things we haven't yet thought of. That's the future for ELT video, the best of which will always aim to achieve the four E's: to *E*ngage, to *E*ntertain, to *E*nthral, and to *E*ducate.

3 LANGUAGE AND LEARNING

3.1 RP R.I.P? Wherever next with pronunciation?

Robin Walker *Escuela Universitaria de Turismo de Asturias, Spain*

Given the widely recognized role of English as a medium for international communication, with non-native speakers of the language now constituting around 80% of the total user population, the validity of RP, GA or any other native-speaker accent as a norm or model is no longer tenable. This talk, therefore, briefly reviewed recent developments with regard to alternative pronunciation goals, before taking a detailed look at Jennifer Jenkins' 'Lingua Franca Core' (LFC).

The LFC is the first attempt to determine pronunciation goals for English as an International Language (EIL). Having established the validity of the Core, the talk went on to examine the implications for teachers working with monolingual groups, the majority situation around the world. Taking Spanish speakers of English as an example, a demonstration was given of how the application of the LFC to traditional lists of problems and priorities (as identified by L1/L2 contrastive analysis) generates new pronunciation goals. A similar 'filtering' can be made of any other traditional L1-specific list, the beneficial effects of this process being that:

- the remaining priorities have been empirically demonstrated to be essential for international intelligibility. In traditional lists, certain priorities respond more to attempts at accent reduction in order to satisfy native-speaker concepts of 'correctness', than to criteria for international communication, where accent is identity.
- the resulting list of priorities is far smaller than traditional alternatives, an important point, given the time dedicated to pronunciation work in the majority of classrooms.
- almost all LFC goals are attainable through classroom teaching, an issue of crucial importance. Too much time has been spent previously on aspects of pronunciation which, whilst learnable outside the classroom, are not teachable within it.

The talk next examined the way in which the substantial step forward the LFC represents in terms of goals, is maximized if the role of the learner's L1 is reconsidered. With monolingual groups, by taking the L1 as the starting point, as opposed to perceiving it as an obstacle in the learner's path, the emphasis is switched away from what students cannot do, or from what is 'missing', and is placed firmly on the usefulness of their mother-tongue or its varieties. Examples were given from the phonology and phonetics of Spanish, French and Brazilian Portuguese as to how a detailed analysis of the L1 actually facilitates achievement of the majority of the goals set out by the LFC.

Finally, the talk examined the supposed superiority of native speakers as instructors. Since our goal is no longer a native-speaker accent, the privileged position of native speakers as models is lost. In addition, non-native speaker teachers with the same L1 as their learners are better situated as instructors, their own successful learning experience enriching the range of techniques and 'tricks' available to them, and making them more sympathetic to possible psychological barriers to performance. Lastly, as accomplished users of English, non-native speaker teachers know exactly what is or is not intelligible to interlocutors.

E-mail: rwalker@las.es

3.2 Understanding 'understanding' in learners' talk: A conversation analytic (CA) approach

Anita Alzamora *University of Salford, England*

Spoken language in the classroom is often analysed from a linguistic point of view and seen primarily as a mentalistic phenomenon. However, another approach initially developed by Sacks (1992) and derived from interactionist sociology, namely Conversation Analysis, suggests seeing talk in the classroom as an interactionally negotiated phenomenon that is socially organised, comprising conversational actions and their serial organisation. This report outlines a case study research project that adopted a CA approach and found that the EGAP seminar participants, regardless of their fluency/accuracy, were using clarification skills and beginning to develop effective ways of taking part in discussions.

While viewing the videotaped seminar discussion, certain language practices involving understanding were noted in some turn taking utterances, and sections of the audio-based recording with these features were transcribed according to CA transcription conventions. These practices were examined to see *how* they were accomplished and defined by the *participants* overtly and collaboratively in context. The students' 'understanding' of prior talk (utterance turns and sequences) emerged as a phenomenon for closer scrutiny.

One data sequence was analysed. It was found that students' talk exemplified the distinction made by Sacks (1969: 140–142) between the conversational actions of 'claims and displays of understanding'. In a claim to understanding a participant avows or implies understanding. However, in a display of understanding a participant demonstrates or shows understanding. Different methods are used: e.g. a token 'yes' or 'OK' in a claim as opposed to a paraphrase of a prior utterance in a display.

Two examples are provided in the data below. In the first, 'A' (line 29) made a claim of not understanding. This referred to the first 28 lines of this extract concerning the nature and constituents of the communist bloc and its alignment with America. However, to the 'SP' (line 30) it is not clear what it is that 'A' does not understand, so the 'SP' repeats the word 'division' to elicit further information from 'A'.

29 A: No I don't understand (che) division
30 SP: Division for [example
31 A: [Some countries with Russia, some countries with
32 America
33 SP: Yeah

In the second example, 'A' (lines 31–32) proposes a display of understanding. It is also a gist formulation on the topic being discussed. 'A' is trying to make sense of the talk. This utterance is the first pair part of an adjacency pair formulation. The second part (line 33) is a confirmation of the proposed formulation. In other words, the 'SP' agrees with 'A's proposed summary of the topic thus far.

There are some practical issues raised by this research about the benefits of using real talk-in-interaction data for teaching/learning and materials development. A closer examination of students' talk (through audio/videotapes and transcriptions) may reveal that learners are already using a wide variety of clarification skills, so it is possible to build upon and extend these skills. Learners can be involved in self-assessment by examining their own talk in context with interactional reference to others. Finally, it might be useful to create a materials bank with examples of learners' talk for developing other discussion skills.

E-mail: Anitamaw@tesco.net

3.3 Communication strategies of non-native speakers' and native speakers' comprehension

Naciye Kunt *Eastern Mediterranean University, Turkey*

People use a variety of communication strategies (CSs) to reach their desired goals. These strategies may be different for first and second language speakers. For example, a learner of a second language may, in the course of conversation, switch to his or her native language or use a cognate when s/he needs to use a word that is not part of active L2 vocabulary. Research was carried out to explore non-native speakers' use of CSs in a foreign language. This is a report of one aspect of the larger study: the factors that contribute to the effectiveness of non-native speakers' CSs.

Data was collected through a story-telling task. The subjects were eight adults (four male and four female) studying at a university in the US. All subjects' first language was Turkish and their English proficiency levels ranged from novice to advanced. They performed a story-telling task in English based on simple pictures. The subjects were audio-taped during the story-telling and these tapes were transcribed; from these transcriptions the most difficult target concepts and communicative behaviours were selected. To find out the extent to which native speakers agree whether or not the subjects' speech production would be correctly understood by native speakers of English, tape-recordings and transcriptions were presented to a group of native speakers. They rated the speech production of the subjects on a scale from one to five (native speaker comprehension ratings).

Findings revealed that native speakers' comprehension was linearly proportional to the Turkish subjects' length of formal English study. That is, the fewer years of study, the lower the native speakers' comprehension ratings and vice versa. The results also indicated that gender and the proficiency level of the subjects had an impact on the use of CSs, i.e. the female subjects used more CSs than the males, and more proficient subjects in English used fewer CSs. These findings may have some implications for foreign language teaching, especially in the areas of lesson planning, language testing, and teaching methodology.

Most language learners are capable of using CSs, and in fact they do employ CSs every now and then, but they may not be able to use the appropriate CSs or they may use ineffective ones in their conversations. If teachers are aware of the CSs that the learners use, they may be able to help learners to choose more appropriate CSs and use them in a more creative and efficient way. Teachers may also help learners in reducing their anxiety when they lack some lexical and grammatical items. They also need to guide learners to build up their confidence and awareness of their language use. Although there has been some controversy regarding the teachability of CSs, I believe that we should teach effective ones in order to assist L2 learners to become better language learners and communicators.

E-mail: naciye@hotmail.com

3.4 Symmetry and asymmetry in job interviews

Zaina A Abdalla Nunes *Catholic University of Sao Paulo and Cultura Inglesa, Brazil*

The general objective of this research was to describe and analyze the discourse of interviews, using the genre of job interviews, and to:

a) motivate ELT professionals to carry on their studies at post-graduate level, investigating language in their fields of work;
b) highlight aspects to be dealt with in ESP lessons when preparing students for the job market: the organization of interviews in terms of topics tackled and questions usually asked;
c) expose practising teachers to samples of job interviews and reflect on what usually happens that could help or hinder the applicant's success.

The analysis developed here was based on Michael Halliday's functional-systemic grammar (1985), where language is seen as a 'social rather than an individual phenomenon', manifested through a text and its environment. It was complemented by ideas from the critical discourse analysts Kress (1989) and Fairclough (1992), and from some Brazilian linguists: Koch (1983), Ilari (1986), Rosa (1992), and Santos (1991).

The *research questions* used to develop such investigation were:

1 How is the genre of job interviews in academic contexts organized?
2 From the point of view of power, how do participants relate to each other?
3 What kinds of questions tend to occur in such interactions and what are their functions?
4 What is the relation between the linguistic markers in the questions and their respective functions, which show an asymmetrical relationship?

Ten interviews were audio-recorded during real-life manifestations of this type of discourse. All the interviewers were teachers of English who held positions as academic co-ordinators. Only one interviewee was a native user of English – the others were Brazilian teachers of English.

In this interaction, the candidate applies for a job as a TEFLer and undergoes an interview as part of the selection process. However, for the interaction to take place, a series of steps must be followed. Four obligatory stages were identified:

1 Opening
2 Asking for and giving information
3 Asking for and giving opinions
4 Closing

Two criteria were used to identify the subdivision of those stages: a *functional* one (Hasan 1989), where the event is organized according to the function each stage performs; a *topical* one, linked to the concept of topic as something constructed once more than one participant contributes to its development. Among the 29 topics noted were: previous experience; attending a training course; salary; availability; teaching methodology.

As regards *power*, the interviewer 'has the option of asserting or disguising it somewhat'. (Kress 1989: 55). Various instances were observed where the interviewers made linguistic choices to minimize or maximize their power. When it alternated between interviewer and interviewee, this happened more intensely through the *content* on the interviewee's part and through the *interaction* itself from the interviewer's side. The intrinsic power of the interviewer did not seem to be exclusively exercised at any point during the interactions studied.

E-mail: abdallanunes@uol.com.br

3.5 Task effects on vocabulary acquisition through reading in EFL

Halina Chodkiewicz *Maria Curie-Skłodowska University, Poland*

Although incidental vocabulary acquisition has been found to be a natural phenomenon accompanying reading, its efficiency is low and difficult to measure, as word knowledge develops in an incremental way. This report presents a part of an empirical study whose goal was to provide more insight into the effects of texts, tasks and learner strategies on vocabulary learning through reading in EFL. The questions addressed were: whether while-reading (promoting comprehension) tasks differentially affected vocabulary acquisition, whether the relationship between text comprehension and vocabulary acquisition was differentially affected by particular task types, and whether vocabulary gains were affected by the level of learners' proficiency.

Study

The subjects, 222 Polish students of the English Department and Teacher Training Colleges, assigned to three balanced groups, were instructed to read three newspaper articles for comprehension, while performing three different tasks: reading the text autonomously ('read only' condition), reading for the main ideas (multiple choice task), and reading for some details (true/false statements), making the target words salient. Whereas the students knew that their reading comprehension was to be checked, they did not expect that a vocabulary test – 240 questions containing 60 words selected from the articles, 4 questions per word sensitive to partial word knowledge, a version of the pre-test they had taken three weeks before – would re-appear as a post-test. By comparing the results of the post-test and the pre-test, vocabulary gains for all the students were established.

Results

All the students were involved in the incidental vocabulary acquisition process; they moved up from an average of 25% of correct answers on the pre-test to 38.6% on the post-test. The difference between the effects of Tasks 1 and 2 on vocabulary gains was significant, that between Tasks 1 and 3 was on the border of significance, while it was insignificant between Tasks 2 and 3. The correlation between the comprehension scores and Tasks 2 and 3 results was 0.44 and 0.37 for all the students, but was far lower for the different language proficiency levels. A higher degree of text comprehension did not affect vocabulary acquisition to the same extent.

Conclusion

Whereas all the students were able to acquire meanings of unfamiliar words, regardless of their initial knowledge of the target words, their vocabulary gains were affected by their language proficiency level. A tentative conclusion is that enhancing reading by means of an activity that directs the learner to identify the main ideas is less profitable for vocabulary acquisition than reading a text for selected information, making the target words salient, and still less profitable than reading the text independently. The relationship between comprehensible input and language acquisition seems to be more complex than Krashen's theory allows. The rate of vocabulary learning seems to be predominantly connected with the type of language input, whereas different ways of promoting text comprehension do not contribute significantly to enhancing the process of vocabulary acquisition from context.

E-mail: hachod@klio.umcs.lublin.pl

3.6 Putting polysemy to work: Corpora and vocabulary projects in ESP

Andy Cresswell *University of Bologna, Italy*

ESP is traditionally assumed to involve the learning of vocabulary restricted to a single occupation or discipline, but in some situations (e.g. technical high schools, cross-disciplinary university language centres) teachers must teach technical vocabulary appropriate to a range of fields. It was hypothesized, first, that much of such 'semi-technical' vocabulary would be polysemic, i.e. a single base form and underlying semantic would assume variations in different fields, and second, that learners could be made aware of such polysemes, and of technical contexts in general, through project work involving 'discovering' polysemes on the British National Corpus (BNC).

In the projects, small groups of learners (in this case advanced) found DIY texts, or operating instructions, and identified in them potential polysemes to follow to their different contexts as listed in BNC concordances, the linguistic aim being to verify the degree of polysemy of each. The learners checked the meaning of each use of the word in dictionaries, noting the field, context and definition in a booklet, together with further definitions of any previously unknown associated words. These glossaries were later supplemented by learning activities such as multiple-choice, multiple-matching, gap-fill and crosswords, which each small group designed and used to peer-teach their polysemes to the other small groups.

During the course of the projects, non-polysemic words were not excluded, provided the aims of verifying the degree of polysemy of each item, and of learning technical vocabulary, were followed. Beyond these points, in fact, autonomy reigned, with learners proposing what words to include in their booklets, what learning activities to provide, and what dictionaries (on-line or in print) to consult. Much of the final outcome was thus negotiated, both between learners and with the teacher, *en route*, as envisaged by Candlin (1987).

End-of-project evaluation (by semi-structured interviews) found learners valued the method, first, as experience of coming to grips with a range of technical contexts, in the sense of processes (some common, e.g. screw/unscrew/screwdriver) and fields (e.g. electronics, pottery); second, because it highlighted the advantages and disadvantages of using various dictionaries and a large general corpus in working with technical words (there was a general move towards preferring native-speaker to learners' dictionaries); third, because they found it pleasant to work autonomously. As for polysemic semi-technical words, a pooling of three successive years of learners' researches resulted in a total of 180 forms[1] verified as semi-technical polysemes, suggesting, perhaps controversially, the usefulness in vocabulary learning of focusing, via corpora, on a limited number of forms across a number of contexts, in addition to the orthodox 'one context, several related forms' approach. Finally, the results confirm the value of autonomous approaches: learners, collectively, can research and compile their own reference lists of generally applicable words; it is not always necessary to derive them pre-digested from published sources, and it is surely good for the quality of their learning if learners discover them for themselves.

E-mail: cresswel@sslmit.unibo.it

Note

[1] Examples: bus, cradle, dress, footprint, head, lip, nipple, plate, port, rib, seam.

3.7 Literacy and foreign language reading

Tony Ridgway *Queen's University of Belfast, Northern Ireland*

Literacy has come to mean a lot more than merely decoding or encoding written text. Interactive approaches to reading emphasize the different relationships between reader and text, and the plural form 'literacies' is an indication of this change. Reading studies focus on skills and strategies, whereas literacy studies focus more on styles and attitudes. What the reader brings to the text beyond cognitive skills affects not only interpretation but also what is done with the text. A modern academic text, for example, may be followed word for word as if it were a sacred text rather than a weapon in the armoury of self-directed learning. Obfuscation of written text has diminished a lot thanks to campaigns such as Plain Words, but still has a long way to go. Mass literacy is a relatively modern phenomenon, and traces of pre-literate or restricted-literate attitudes towards written text remain.

The foregoing are examples of restricted literacy practices. Diachronically, there is a progression from illiteracy to functional literacy to restricted literacy to mass literacy, but these are also all present synchronically. So we still have illiterates, and those who read or record only in order to carry out their trade, and people like lawyers who read and write within a restricted sphere which others do not understand. Many of the students who come to us (in particular Chinese) come from countries where mass literacy has arrived only relatively recently; they may still have some of the attitudes towards text associated with restricted literacy, and need to learn how to approach a modern academic text, for example, as well as how to decode it. The importance of this is that unless they do learn how to approach it, they will probably not read it at all, since the most ever-present option in reading is that of abandoning the text.

The multivalency of 'literacies' is also reflected in ESP approaches towards reading (notably including EAP), where background knowledge and lexical specialization can combine to overcome linguistic difficulties, a process more akin to problem-solving than to fluent reading.

The concept of 'literacies' may appear to problematize the concept of 'transfer of skills/strategies', which many believe happens in reading once a certain level of linguistic proficiency has been reached. This need not be the case, however, if we return to the distinction made above between skills and strategies, on the one hand, and styles and attitudes on the other. There is therefore an argument for making a distinction between literacy and literacies, rather than regarding the latter term as a better description, as the so-called New Literacy does. L2 literacy is a language problem which all language teachers must face at lower levels; L2 literacies continue to cause problems, especially in the academic sphere, but potentially in any domain, at higher levels, and has something to do with the phenomenon of the Chinese students who take off from Beijing at Upper Intermediate Level and land at Heathrow as Lower Intermediates.

E-mail: t.ridgway@qub.ac.uk

3.8 What's the point? Narrative structure, L2 comprehension and working memory

Catherine Walter *Freelance, England*

In ELT classes we 'teach' learners to recognize the main points in a reading passage. But if the learners are already literate in their first language (L1), they recognize these points already. Do we need to teach them to do it in their second language (L2)?

Skilled reading comprehension is characterized by the building of an orderly mental representation, or structure, of the text being read. 'Orderly' here means well-integrated and hierarchical. Incoming information is fitted into the developing structure and related to what has gone before. In skilled structure-building, main points are recalled better than subsidiary points, because, in a hierarchical structure, a main point is activated every time an element is integrated below it in the hierarchy, and more activation means better recall.

An orderly mental structure means that a comprehender can self-monitor, and realize when a new element is anomalous. Skilled comprehenders will be more sensitive to main-point anomalies than to subsidiary-point anomalies. In a first experiment, I measured the self-monitoring ability in L1 (French) and L2 (English) of two groups of adolescents, a lower-intermediate group and an upper-intermediate group. Their task was to detect anomalies in a series of nine texts in each language. In L1 both groups detected anomalies reliably, and detected main-point anomalies better than subsidiary-point anomalies. But in L2 only the upper-intermediate group reliably detected anomalies, even though the texts corresponded well to their proficiency level.

A second experiment took L1 and L2 measures of these learners' Working Memory (WM). WM is not a simple recall ability, but a system of mechanisms by which people process and maintain in an accessible form the information they need for performing complex cognitive tasks. We know that WM is related to reading comprehension skill in L1. The WM measure in this experiment combined 1) a processing task: reading a list of sentences and deciding if each was 'logical'; and 2) a recall task: remembering the last word of each sentence. (An example of an 'illogical' sentence: *The sofa jumped on the dog.*) Longer and longer lists of sentences were presented, until recall became unreliable. Scoring combined judgment reliability, reaction time and recall.

There was a small difference between the two groups for L1 WM, but a significantly much greater distance for L2 WM. So the learners who have significantly lower L2 WM are the same as those who are poor at L2 structure building. Plotting all the WM scores against all the scores for the first experiment showed a higher correlation between WM and anomaly detection when 'the going got tough': that is, in L2 and for the lower-intermediate group.

What does this mean for the classroom? L1-literate lower intermediate learners do have trouble distinguishing main points in texts, but trying to teach them to do so is not the best use of our time. We should concentrate on building grammatical and lexical proficiency, while exposing learners to short extensive reading texts, until they are ready to transfer their L1 reading comprehension skills to L2.

E-mail: cwalter@place-farm.demon.co.uk

3.9 Objectives and methodological issues in translation practice

Gloria Sampaio *Catholic University of Sao Paulo, Brazil*

Translation practice lessons comprise short- and long-term objectives. Short-term objectives have to do with dealing with a particular source text in a given classroom situation, and producing an adequate and acceptable rendering of it into the other language, taking into account, among other things, the type of text, the purpose of the translation, the target public, together with due consideration of textual norms and literary canons in force. Cultural knowledge, mastery of the languages involved, along with sensibility, inspiration, imagination and creativity – or the lack of any of these – are bound to surface in the process there and then.

Long-term objectives have to do with awareness-raising, regarding not only the aspects mentioned above, but also theoretical, ethical and socio-political issues, such as the role of the translator, the question of authorship and responsibility towards the texts involved. Referring to the importance of theoretical considerations, Newmark (1998: 36–37) reminds us that what translation theory can do is 'show the student all that is or may be involved in the translation process and offer principles and guidelines, after considering which, he makes his choices and decisions', and that it 'precipitates a methodology concerned with making the translator pause and think'.

This overall scenario of objectives demands close attention and calls for specific methodological responses to provide the necessary means and conditions for students to expand their repertoire, cultivate their sensibility and nurture their creativity.

Repertoire should account for the building-up, enlarging and refining of linguistic competence and performance, the broadening of cultural horizons, the adoption of strategies that will foster the development of specific translation abilities and skills, and the enhancement of previous and/or newly acquired knowledge of the very many aspects the translation process entails. Sensitization should be achieved by a continuous awareness-raising process which leads students to perceive, feel and identify the more obvious or more subtle difficulties imposed by a given translation task. Creativity, which encompasses the exercise of imagination, intuition and inspiration, should represent the cornerstone of successful problem-solving in translation.

A well-conducted translation practice lesson should then necessarily be based on methodological decisions that take into account all these elements, which, combined, will provide students with adequate education and training. Thus stimulated and equipped, they will be ready to meet the difficulties and challenges presented by the multi-faceted 'reality' of both source and target texts, considered in their more restricted or wider scope.

E-mail: gloria_sampaio@hotmail.com

3.10 Dark horses and foregone conclusions: Idiom, collocation and cliché

Antoinette Moses *Freelance, England*

> *And most wonderful of all are words, and how they make friends with one another, being oft associated...* O Henry

Teaching idioms forms an important part of language education. Indeed, a command of idiomatic English is what all EFL teachers hope that students will acquire, and collocations form the backbone of the lexical approach. But how can advanced students learn to differentiate between a useful collocation and a cliché? And how can teachers help students to write English without using clichés?

First, I wanted to examine collocations. Michael Lewis (2000) lists 20 different forms of collocation, from discourse markers and fixed phrases to proverbs, but for the purposes of this talk, I pared these down to around six. These were:

- noun + noun — greenhouse effect, market economy
- adjective + noun — mindless violence, heavy heart
- verb + noun — have dinner, run a race
- verb + adverb — talk softly, fall heavily
- adverb + verb — flatly refuse, flagrantly deny
- adverb + adjective — bitterly disappointing, utterly humiliating

It was interesting to see that some of these collocations were more likely to lend themselves to clichés than others. In particular, *verb + adverb* was much less likely to be a cliché than the reversed *adverb + verb* – a subject for further research, I believe.

Secondly, I wanted to examine the nature of cliché. The word originally comes from a French printing term for copying woodcuts and began its metaphorical use as a stereotyped expression at the end of the nineteenth century. The Oxford English Dictionary quotes '...a hatred of clichés [and] of the outworn phrase' from *Longman's Magazine* of 1892. The *LTP Dictionary of Selected Collocations* collocates 'cliché' with *meaningless, stale* and *well-worn*. I could see no difficulty with 'well-worn'. We all use expressions for things that happen frequently, e.g. *It's raining*. 'Stale' was borderline and 'meaningless' revealed the problem. Clichés were frequently phrases used so often that they had become meaningless. Often, too, as I showed, they were tautologies.

> She sat in the hot sun with a glass of cold iced tea in her hand while the soft murmur of the pounding surf echoed faintly in her ears.

The cumulative effect of all these tautologies creates a text that is trite and unimaginative. Every image in this sentence hasn't just been said before – it's been said often, so often that you could guess which word was missing if I took out the adjectives and adverbs.

I ended my talk with an exercise used in creative writing workshops in which teacher and students create (and map) a fictional village. This leads to a writing task beginning: 'What can I tell you about... (name of village)?' The description includes things seen, heard and smelled. I then read two descriptive passages (by Rosamund Pilcher and Penelope Lively) to illustrate how generalized description can lead to cliché, while specific, detailed description does not.

E-mail: amoses@btinternet.com

3.11 'You shouldn't say that': Swearing

Andrew Walkley *University of Westminster, England*

Language teaching is a political act, and this is particularly true when it comes to swearing, which tends to be written out of most EFL discussions. For instance, in the *Cobuild Concise English Dictionary*, there is a glaring gap between 'fuchsia' and 'fuddy-duddy'. Similar censorship occurs in the many talks on real English and corpora, where the question of the supposed dangers of native speaker models is often side-stepped with claims of 'cleaning up' corpus data. In the classroom, students are all too often simply told that such language is taboo. For those who do say and/or teach F-words, they are a love which dare not speak its name. Teachers can be made to feel they're 'dumbing down', or somehow corrupting students. They may even feel their jobs are at risk. Indeed, one delegate told me she could not even admit to her colleagues to having attended my talk on the matter!

Nevertheless, most arguments given for excluding swear words, such as students picking them up anyway, students possibly misusing them, and students possibly sounding strange are, in fact, arguments which deny the possibility of teaching itself. It is difficult to imagine the same being said of a phrase such as 'Of course'! Such arguments also assume native/non-native speaker (NS/NNS) interaction, whereas the majority of conversations are between non-natives. Learners rarely sound strange to themselves! Indeed, many may feel very native-like when they speak, and this can be highly motivating. What governs their use in all conversations is a universal understanding of 'tabooness' (despite the fact that the precise nature of this tabooness differs from language to language).

Furthermore, those who worry about the dangers of NNS swearing over-emphasize the negative aspects of swearing. In reality, the vast majority of swearing is not aggressive or angry (although students should not be denied access to the words used to express such emotions), but rather a means of bonding, and a form of language play. Indeed, it could be argued that excluding swear words is bad teaching in that it presents a distorted view of the language. Exclusion diminishes the spectrum of register and thus the centre ground, which most students occupy, shifts to the right. While this may please those who see themselves as prescribers of what is linguistically good or bad, it is untruthful. It means much language is then treated as slang or rude when it actually isn't, and also excludes other subjects which fail to be unremittingly middle class. In contrast, teaching swearing opens up new areas of lexis and acknowledges the legitimacy of students' own complex linguistic desires.

I advocate a cross-cultural approach to the subject of swearing, teaching the words as they arise and – occasionally – as lexical sets. However, teaching swearing also requires teachers to not be embarrassed and sometimes to adopt less hierarchical teacher roles. I also believe in description not prescription, 'can' over 'shouldn't', and knowledge over ignorance. In short, I believe in education in its fullest sense.

E-mail: Macu.andrew@ukgateway.net

3.12 Plenary: Children's rights, assessment and the digital portfolio: Is there a common denominator?

Kari Smith

Introduction

I would like to start my presentation by giving you a small test. This is a test given to children at 12 years of age in a European country, and their future education depends on the score they get. Based on the test score, the 12-year-olds are selected for various streams of education available in their country. I do not suppose you will have any problems answering the questions, as the test is for children at the end of primary school. (Even though I am sure you do not need to look at the answers, I have put them at the end of the paper, just for self-checking!)

1 What was achieved by the Augsburg Peace Treaty?
2 Define and give an example of an indirect reciprocal sentence.
3 How many faces, edges and vertices does a hexahedron have?
4 What are the main terrestrial biomes?
5 Who organised the 1885 Berlin Congress? What was decided by it?
6 What is elision?

(Esteve, 2000)

These questions are taken from national exams administered to all children in that country, and the test is taken under time pressure. If the child fails to achieve the required score, s/he is considered an academic failure, and already at this stage the doors to academic studies are closed. The child's future has been decided.

The above is an example of how decisions about children and their future are made mainly based on their ability to reproduce important information.

This phenomenon is not new. In 1883 the Norwegian writer Alexander L Kielland wrote a book called *Poison*. It tells the story of Markus, a specially gifted child who did not survive school. He died because he could not take the suppression of his teachers, who did not accept, understand or even try to understand his brilliant mind. His life withered, and the teachers did not see what was happening, but blamed him for not adjusting to school.

Another famous Norwegian, Henrik Ibsen, valued personal truth beyond everything, and he saw it as school's main responsibility to strengthen independent thinking. He did not live to see this being put into practice and I am not so sure that he would have been happy with some of today's educational systems. One hundred and fifty years later, in his plenary talk at the IATEFL 2000 conference in Dublin, Dr Tony Humphreys compared the individual child to an extraordinary pearl which is so valuable that the society and the child her/himself keep it hidden. Little seems to have changed since Kielland's and Ibsen's time.

Convention on the Rights of the Child (20.11.1989)

The need to protect the individual child and her/his individuality has been recognised by world society, which in 1989 found the problem serious enough to create a United Nations Convention on the Rights of the Child. This paper discusses some of the paragraphs of the Convention in the light of what happens in school, and more specifically in assessing children's achievements and learning:

§ 3

The child's best interest must be a primary concern in all actions and decisions affecting children taken by adults and organisations.

- *States must ensure that their institutions and services meet the standards and have the staffing required to achieve this end.*

Questions that come to mind when reading this paragraph include:

- Do schools have sufficient facilities to make decisions where children are of primary concern?
- Is the teaching staff sufficiently qualified, or do teachers teach without proper qualifications and repeated quality assurance?
- Is large-scale testing and selection at an early age (any age?) in the best interest of the child or maybe it is in the best interest of the society?

I am not in a position to answer these questions, but I find it important to ask the questions and to think of how the situation is in our personal educational settings.

§ 12

The child who is capable of forming his or her views has the right to express those views freely in all matters affecting the child, the views being given due weight in accordance with the child's age and maturity.

Questions that need to be asked in relation to this paragraph are:

- Are the children involved in making choices regarding what to learn?
- Are they involved in making choices regarding how to be assessed?
- Do they have a say when they are being placed in levelled study groups?
- How widespread is the use of self-assessment?

In short, do we listen to what children have to say regarding matters that affect them in school? Again, I invite you to think of how the situation is in your own school and in your own classrooms.

§ 13

The child shall have the right to freedom of expression; this right shall include freedom to seek, receive and impart information and ideas of all kinds, regardless of frontiers, either orally, in writing or in print, in the form of art, or through any media of the child's choice.

Do we act according to this paragraph when the majority of tests given in school are pencil and paper tests, or when we use uniform assessment instruments for all children? If tests are designed in such a way that there is a pre-decided correct answer to all questions, where then is the freedom to impart information and ideas? The issues raised in paragraph thirteen leave teachers and parents with much food for thought about how testing and assessment are carried out in various educational settings.

The last paragraph I have chosen to present in this paper is:

§ 29

Education of the child shall be directed to:

- *Develop personality, talents, and mental and physical abilities to their fullest potential.*

In my understanding, this means that we need to see learners as different individuals with different talents and abilities. Assessment is part of education, so the differences should also be taken into consideration when the child is being assessed. It is a question related to the issue of internal and external fairness in assessment.

External and internal fairness

If all learners are assessed in a similar way, and there is similar treatment of all learners, *external fairness* is being used. This happens when all the pupils are given the same test and it is marked according to a fixed answer key. The child behind the test paper is of no importance; the content of the test paper is the only concern.

Internal fairness means that the learner's work is assessed in the light of the context in which it has been produced, and if a group of learners, or an individual learner, were disadvantaged at the time of performance, this is taken into consideration when the performance is being assessed (Leach, Neutze and Zepke 1999).

There are certain situations which require external fairness only, especially when a person's professional skills are being assessed. I would certainly not feel safe in a plane with a pilot who had been found unreliable in stress situations, and this disadvantage had been taken into consideration when he was given his pilot's licence. I would not want to undergo surgery carried out by a surgeon who has a shaky hand, but who had worked so hard during training that he deserved to be given his licence. So there are situations in life in which external fairness is essential.

However, in school, with children who are developing, who are not yet given professional responsibilities such as a pilot's licence, with children who are going through a process of learning about themselves, their talents and abilities, do we not need to take their differences into consideration? According to paragraph 29 in the Convention on the Child's Rights, we have to do so.

Assessment paradigms

The issue of what is meant by external and internal fairness can be explained by looking at assessment in light of various assessment paradigms. Linda Mabry in her book *Portfolio plus – a critical guide to alternative assessment* (1999) discusses three assessment paradigms; the psychometric, the contextualised and the personalised (ipsative) paradigms:

Psychometric	**Contextual**	**Personal**
Standardised in content and administration	Curriculum-sensitive and group-sensitive	Student-sensitive: content, setting and time vary
Objective items and formats	Objective and subjective items and formats	Subjective items and formats. Student involved in selection
External marking (machine)	Teacher marking	Teacher marking
No self-assessment	Self-assessment important	Self-assessment essential
Summative, no feedback beyond score	Formative use of results. Can be used summatively	Formative use of results. Can be used summatively

(Mabry 1999)

The psychometric paradigm serves purposes of external fairness, whereas the two other paradigms, contextual and ipsative, serve purposes of internal fairness. The contextualised paradigm looks at the individuality of the group and in the context of teaching, whereas the ipsative paradigm looks at the individuality of each learner, and how the individual learner progresses in comparison to her/himself. My claim is that when professional skills are assessed for high-stakes selection purposes, the psychometric paradigm seems to be more suitable, but when the rights of the individual child and the child's best interest are of concern, other assessment paradigms need to be applied.

The instructional encounter

The use of different assessment paradigms in education leads to the question of how teachers view teaching, learning and assessment. Are these three processes viewed as separate, or are they viewed as one integrated process? The view taken in this paper is that the three activities integrate in an ongoing process, which can be called the instructional encounter. The concept of the instructional encounter is illustrated in the following model:

The instructional encounter

1st layer:

choice of task → first draft → revision → final product

2nd layer:

guidance in choice of task → feedback → feedback → summative assessment

↖ ↑ ↗

formative assessment

3rd layer:

reason for choice → reflection on content – reflection on process → self-assessment

(4th layer):

teacher's reflections

The learner is given a choice of tasks, and s/he makes a first attempt at the task, which s/he later revises until s/he feels happy with it, and decides to hand in the final version. That is the first layer of the instructional encounter.

The second layer is related to the teacher. The teacher guides the learner in choosing tasks, but does not make the final decision, which remains with the child. The teacher provides formative feedback on the various versions of the child's work, and the child makes revisions based on the teacher's formative, informative feedback. Peers can also be involved in giving feedback to the learner, and all this is taken into consideration when summative assessment of the product is given. Teaching means, in this case, providing formative feedback and guiding the child in her/his individual learning process. Learning, teaching and assessment are thus integrated into one process.

The third layer is the child's reflection, self-awareness of the learning process. The child is asked to reflect on why s/he chose to work on the task, and also to reflect on the content of the task, the quality of the product, as well as on the learning process. This reflective process helps the child develop the skill of self-assessment, which is seen as essential to becoming an active and independent learner. It is also one of the child's rights (see §13 above), and is an integral part of the contextualised and personalised assessment paradigms.

The fourth layer in the instructional encounter is related to the teacher's reflection and learning about the learning process of the individual child and about the instructional encounter with this specific child. This will be further discussed later in this paper.

In the 'instructional encounter', therefore, we can say that there is an integration of learning, teaching and assessment, which takes place when the situation demands it. Furthermore, there is a combination of formative and summative assessment, of teacher-, peer- and self-assessment. The instructional encounter is carried out with the individual learner and serves ipsative assessment purposes.

The portfolio

The theory described in the above is not very useful unless it is possible to put it into practice. So, how can this be done? The best tool I know of is the portfolio, which can be defined as 'a purposeful collection of a student's work over a period of time'.

There are many forms and faces of the portfolio, and I do not want to say that the framework proposed in this paper is the right one or the best one. A portfolio is like a tailor-made dress. It has to fit the context in which it is being used, which means the teaching situation, the subject, the age of the pupils, the individual learner and the teacher. However, this is a framework for the portfolio that I have found useful with younger learners in school as well as with university students.

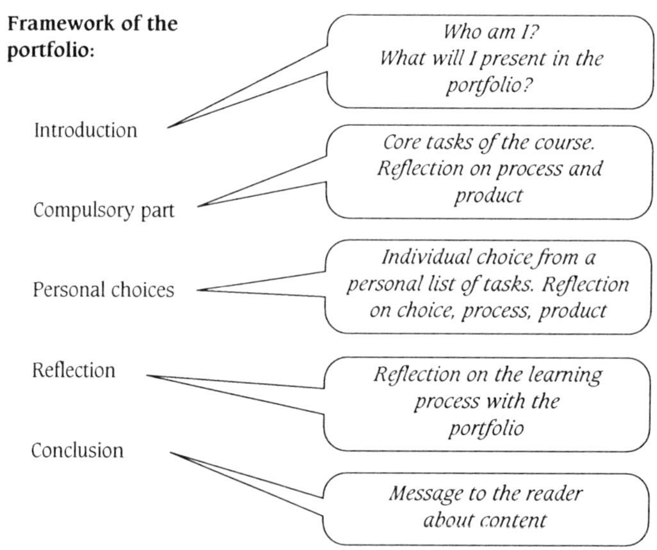

The framework of the portfolio presented here is one which can be used for learning as well as for assessment purposes.

The portfolio has a compulsory part, which includes tasks all learners have to do. These activities reflect the core part of the course or the unit on which the learners compile a portfolio. These are mainly decided by the teacher. The tasks included in the personal choice are many and varied, and some might even be suggested by the individual pupil. All tasks in this part of the portfolio are also related to the course or unit, but the child chooses what to work on.

Each task has to be completed by reflection on the learning process as well as on the content and quality of the product as viewed by the learner. Peers can also be invited to write comments if the class atmosphere allows for it.

The teacher develops a learning dialogue with each learner (second layer of the instructional encounter), in which the main aim is to work with the child at a level that suits her/him, improving the level as the learning dialogue develops. The teacher starts off the learning dialogue at the level which the learner presents in the first draft of the task. The level will naturally differ from child to child.

The digital portfolio

There is much revision and rewriting when working with a portfolio, and this might weaken the child's stamina for dealing with the tasks. However, a solution to simplify the whole process is to use the computer and to work with the individual child on a digital portfolio. Here are some of the advantages of the digital portfolio:

- The computer simplifies the learning dialogue for the teacher and the learner. There is less copy-work and more real revision.
- Feedback is personalised and focused on a specific problem.
- The computer is, in itself, motivating for many learners, and for some, it is even more natural to work with a computer than with a pen or pencil and paper.
- The computer allows for interaction with electronic corpora, which serves the need to use resource material when this is required (instead of having to run to the library to find it).

It is not necessary to work with the computer in order to work with portfolios, but it simplifies the whole process for everybody involved, and it is therefore recommended if the facilities allow for it.

The case of Nathan

The last part of this paper exemplifies an instructional encounter carried out with the help of the digital portfolio.

Nathan is a young learner of English, ten years old. His first language is Hebrew, and he is now in his second year of learning English. Last year he had two weekly hours of English, which were mainly spent in creating a basic oral vocabulary and teaching reading and writing in the English alphabet. For Hebrew-speaking learners (and many others, including Arab learners of English) one of the first major difficulties is to get used to reading from left to right instead of from right to left, and to reading in a language which has vowels as part of the alphabet.

Nathan was given the task of writing a short essay in English about something that occupied his mind.

This is Nathan's first draft:

Hi my name is Nathan and I in class 5. I like to swim.
This story is on my komptuishn. This komptuishn is vare inopportune to me.
It's inopportune to me beaks waif I suksid I'm going hap to national shmpion ship, and in lost heir I suksid to do dut.
I vary skier from this komptuishn beaks I don't be shor I'm going hap.
But I swim good to me.
And no I wailing to the results.
And I wail talk to yoh if I suksid.

It might be difficult to understand what Nathan really wants to say in his written essay. When the text is read out, however, it becomes a coherent text in which Nathan introduces himself, and talks about his concern as to whether he will qualify for the national swimming championship or not. He also tells the teacher that he will keep her informed about the results. The following is the learning dialogue that the teacher started with Nathan.

Hi my name is Nathan and I in class 5. I like to swim.
This story is on my ***komptuishn****. This komptuishn is* ***vare inopportune*** *to me.*
It's inopportune to me ***beaks waif*** *I suksid I'm going hap to national shmpion ship, and in lost heir I suksid to do dut.*
I vary skier from this komptuishn beaks I don't be shor I'm going hap.
But I swim good to me.
And no I waiting to the results.
And I wail talk to yoh if I suksid.

Hi, Nathan,

Thank you for sharing with me how you feel about the **competition**. I understand it is **very important** to you **because if** you succeed, you will qualify for the national championship. It is okay to be tense. I am looking forward to hearing if you succeed to qualify for the championship.

Jane

Nathan, try to use my letter when revising your story.

Jane, the teacher, chose not to correct all mistakes. Instead she decided to relate to the content of the essay by using correct language. Nathan is not expected to have a perfect version next time, but he is expected to present an improved version of the essay.

This is what Nathan came up with the second time:

> *Hi my name is Nathan and I in class 5. I like to swim.*
> *This story is* ***on (1)*** *my competition. This competition is very important to me. It's* ***inopportune (2)*** *to me because if I succeed, I'm will qualify for the national championship, and* <u>*in lost heir I succeed to do dut. (3)*</u>
> *I vary tense* ***from (4)*** *this competition* ***beaks (5)*** <u>*I don't be shor I'm going up (6)*</u> *But I* <u>*swim good to me (7)*</u>.
> *And* ***no (8)*** *I ? (9) waiting* ***to (10)*** *the results.*
> *And I* ***wail (11)*** *talk to you if I succeed.*

> Hi, Nathan, This is much better. Let us see what we can do to help you learn more:
> **1. In English we say 'a story about something'.**
> **2. Look carefully how you spell this word.**
> <u>3. Please change to: 'last year I succeeded to do that.'</u>
> **4. You are tense 'before' this ...**
> **5. Look carefully how you spell this word.**
> <u>6. You are not sure you will ... (see how you say this)</u>
> <u>7. You swam as well you could.</u>
> **8. Not 'no', but 'now'. What is the difference?**
> **9. What is missing here?**
> **10. You are waiting 'for' the results.**
> **11. How do you spell this word?**

There is a clear improvement in Nathan's essay in this version, but there is still much that can be improved. However, the learning dialogue seems to be efficient, and Jane decided to be more focused in her comments on this version.[1]

In the meantime Jane is making her own reflections on Nathan's work and what she needs to do to guide him in the future. This is the fourth level of the instructional encounter.

- Nathan is capable of expressing himself
- His spelling is weak
- He has problems with use of *be* and *do* as auxiliaries
- He learns from comments
- He makes good revisions
- His focused learning weakens
- Are his corrections copied?

Jane has listed points she has learned about Nathan's learning from his work which help her decide how she wants to continue to work with Nathan in the future.

- Work on spelling and style
- Work on structure
- Ongoing revisions
- Work on self-discovery of problems

The learning dialogue with Nathan has enabled Jane to work out a personal study plan with Nathan, which she can put into action in the next portfolio assignment.

Let me now get back to Nathan and take a look at his final product, which has been revised based on the guidelines he received from Jane.

Hi my name is Nathan and I'm in class 5. I like to swim.
This story is about my competition. This competition is very important to me.
It's important to me because if I succeed, I will qualify for the national championship, and last year I succeeded to do that.
I'm very tense before this competition because I'm not sure I will qualify.
But I swam as well you could.
And now I'm waiting for the results.
And I will talk to you if I succeed.

As you can see, the essay is not perfect, yet this version is much better than the rough version which was the starting point for the learning dialogue Jane initiated with Nathan. Through ongoing formative assessment, Nathan was able to improve his essay until he, as well as Jane, felt that this specific assignment had been completed. The summative assessment given to Nathan was not in the form of a grade, but in a letter that related to the content of the essay as well to the learning process and the language:

Hi, Nathan,
I really hope you will qualify, but if not, you did your best, and that is most important. You have also done a good job with this assignment. The improvement is noticeable. You are able to tell a story in English. Try to remember that we cannot translate directly from Hebrew to English. You need to think of English grammar when you write.
Jane

I have given an example above of a learning dialogue that takes place in an instructional encounter. Learning, teaching and assessment are combined into one ongoing process, and it is, at times, difficult to differentiate among the three. The example also includes illustration of the fourth layer, which relates to the teacher's reflections on the child's work, and how she plans her future teaching with this specific pupil.

However, one layer has not yet been illustrated, and that is the third layer, the child's meta-cognitive process in which he not only reflects on the process, but also takes on self-assessment of the process as well as of the end product. Nathan does not have the language proficiency to write his reflections in English, and Jane has therefore told him to do so in Hebrew, his first language. Her aim with this task is not to improve his English, but to help Nathan understand himself as a learner, and to help him realise that in the end, the most important thing is that he is aware of what he has learned. In the following there are two examples of Nathan's reflections, translated into English. The first piece relates to the question of choice and the second relates to the learning outcome.

Why did I choose to write this story? I chose to work on this story because at that time I was very worried about the swimming competition. However, at the end I did not succeed in swimming as well as I wanted (I did not qualify for the championship).
What did I learn? From the revisions I learned that I have to remember to write *I'm*. Before that I often wrote only *I*. *Will* needs to be written with a double *l*, and not only one *l*. These were the most important things. I did not learn many new words, I just used words I haven't used before (such as *qualify* and *championship*). The assignment helped me learn how to write words like *competition*. I feel the revisions helped me with my English. I think the final product is fine.

Nathan is honest in talking about his feelings, and he also shows that he was a good sport when, in the end, he did not qualify for the national championship. He is pleased with the final product of the writing task, though, and seems able to pinpoint what he learned from working on this. He did a lot of work, and in the end he finds it has helped him learn more English. This is the third layer of the instructional encounter, the layer in which the learner is invited and encouraged to look at his work and at himself 'from the outside' with a reflective orientation.

Jane concludes the learning dialogue with Nathan by relating to his reflections:

> Nathan, I'm sorry you did not qualify, but there is always another chance. Keep up the good work.
>
> Jane

> Nathan, I'm happy to see you have learned some important things. I hope you will go on using words you understand. Try to use a dictionary for spelling.
>
> Jane

Jane's summative assessment on Nathan's product is part of the fourth layer.

Nathan, essay on swimming:

- The final product is good.
- He understands and applies comments in his revisions.
- He is able to define his personal learning product.
- His passive vocabulary seems to be richer than his active vocabulary.
- His oral fluency seems to be better than his written fluency.

– I need to work with him on the written language and on basic accuracy.
– There seems to be a heavy L1 influence in his use of English.

Problems

Nathan's case is a rather straightforward and simple example of how the instructional encounter is practised. Learning, teaching, assessment and reflection interact in an ongoing process by means of the learning dialogue which develops between the child and the teacher. It is, however, necessary to examine some of the problems involved in working with the individual learner in such a personalised way:

- **Time**: It is time-consuming for the teacher as well as for the learner. The dialogue is intensive and personalised, and it is more time-consuming than marking objective discrete-item tests. So, it would be impossible for teachers to work like this all the time. It is, however, possible to work with an individual learning dialogue on a certain number of assignments during the course. Each assignment takes time, because it is quality work instead of quantity work. Personally I believe that there is a tendency in many teaching situations to teach in order to cover material, due to external pressures, instead of making sure that children learn the material.
- **Facilities**: Not all schools have the necessary facilities to let children work with computers in school, and it cannot always be expected that the child has a computer at home. Computers are, however, becoming more common, and it is, I suppose, only a question of time before they become basic school equipment. The portfolio and the learning dialogue do not, however, have to be digital, yet the computer simplifies the whole process. When using a computer, there is less straightforward copy-work, the child can easily save old drafts and revise new drafts, and the teacher can add her comments to the child's file, and save them and her personal reflections in a separate file for each child. The whole process becomes very much more efficient, neater and more feasible with the help of a computer.

- **Computer knowledge**: Not all children and all teachers are sufficiently computer-literate to work with the digital computer. However, if the facilities are there, the main problems do not seem to lie with the children, but with the teachers. We are, at present, in a transitional period, in which some pupils are more computer-literate than some teachers are, and this creates a complex situation. There are two solutions to this problem: 1) Teachers make sure they become computer-literate. 2) Teachers are open to learning from children. This is already problematic in many educational settings and teaching situations without teachers being computer-literate.
- **Acceptance by authorities, parents and decision makers**: Much of the present assessment system is based on psychometric testing and it might be difficult to convince stakeholders of education that different, more contextualised and ipsative assessment paradigms are better suited for children in school. We still have a long way to go before society is ready to incorporate the rights children have to develop their individual talents and to express themselves in ways they have chosen.
- **Teachers' beliefs about learning, teaching and assessment**: Research on teachers' beliefs suggests that it is very difficult to change teachers' beliefs (Pajares 1992; Richardson 1996, among others). The implementation of children's rights through the use of a digital portfolio goes against what many teachers believe teaching and learning is all about. *'Teaching is telling, learning is remembering, and assessment is testing what has been remembered from what has been told.'*

It will take more than a plenary talk at an IATEFL conference and a paper like this to change teachers' beliefs. Those of us who favour changes in education need to accept the fact that is a long process, which needs to start with pre-service teacher education, as well as extensive in-service training for practising teachers.

Conclusions

In the title of this paper I asked if there is a common denominator for children's rights, assessment and the digital portfolio. Throughout, by referring to specific articles in the 1989 UN Convention, I have tried to argue that some assessment practices violate the Rights of the Child. I have suggested that learning, teaching and assessment create an instructional encounter, in which the individual child makes choices and learns by becoming engaged in a learning dialogue encouraged by the teacher. An example of such a learning dialogue carried out on a computer has been included to illustrate an instructional encounter. The learning dialogue involves the child as a person, as a learner, and as a language learner, and the teacher responds to the learner at all three levels.

So, my answer to the title question is a firm YES: there is a common denominator between children's rights, assessment and the digital portfolio. The common denominator is *education and care for children.*

Note

[1] Editor's note: The words shown in bold and underlined originally appeared in different colours.

Answers to the test questions

1 The end of the religious wars between Catholics and Protestants.
2 One in which the subject both perform and receive an action, and the reciprocal pronoun is the indirect object, e.g. *John and Mary kiss each other.*
3 6 faces, 12 edges, and 8 vertices.
4 Different types of region where life exists: tundra, steppe, jungle, savanna, desert.
5 Germany (Bismarck). The distribution of Africa among the European powers.
6 The joining of one vowel with another, forming a single metric syllable, when in the same verse the final syllable of one word ends in a vowel, and the first syllable of the following word begins with one.

(Esteve, 2000)

References

Esteve J M (2000) Culture in school: assessment and the content of education. In *European Journal of Teacher Education, 23/1*, 5–19

Kielland A L (1971) (written in 1883) *Gift*, Oslo Gyldendal Norsk Forlag

Leach L, G Neutze & N Zepke (1999) Learners' perceptions of assessment: tension between philosophy and practice. In *Testing, Evaluation and Assessment (TEA) SIG Newsletter*, No. 1, 1999

Mabry L (1999) *Portfolio plus – a critical guide to alternative assessment*. Thousand Oaks, Corwin Press, Inc.

Pajares M (1992) Teachers' beliefs and educational research: Cleaning up a messy construct. In *Review of Educational Research, 62*, 307.

Richardson V (1996) The role of attitudes and beliefs in learning to teach. In Sikula J (Ed.) *Handbook of research on teacher education.* New York: Macmillan

United Nations (1989) *Convention on the rights of the child.* Geneva, Switzerland: Office of the United Nations High Commissioner for Human Rights

4 LANGUAGE IN THE CLASSROOM

4.1 Babies and bathwater: Mother tongue in the classroom revisited

Olha Madylus *The British Council, Greece*

Using students' L1 in the classroom is no longer considered a crime. Atkinson (1987) argues that translation may be students' preferred learning style. According to Bolitho (1983), humanist teachers should allow self-expression in L1. Atkinson also proposes that classroom activities like checking comprehension and explaining methodology can be effectively done in L1.

All this sounds great to me, but does this apply when the students are five or six years old? I think not.

- Not only do young children not have the language to talk about language, they have not yet developed those sophisticated skills of comparing and contrasting two or more language systems.
- We must think not about language that children comprehend, but about the *message they are decoding*. Often the basis of this decoding is minimally linguistic and based more on prediction derived from earlier experience, visual clues and the vital information that is conveyed through intonation, pitch, volume etc. They can infer, guess, make logical assumptions and imagine. Because they are good at decoding, young children have no problems understanding when their teacher:
  - happily accepts their use of L1, but replies in English
  - illustrates language clearly
  - models activities and games
  - has routines and activity types that students are comfortable with
  - uses story as a medium for language presentation and practice
- Many Primary level courses advise teachers to explain language and activities in L1. The danger in doing this is that:
  a) students get confused by metalanguage and complex explanations
  b) L1 takes over and English becomes a subject for study like Maths
  c) time allocated to the Primary English lesson is eaten away and children actually hear and process very little English
  d) it is hard for the teacher to distinguish between when it is or is not appropriate to use L1 or English
  e) students will automatically tune in to it and ignore the English
  f) the activity is still hard to do, because it's easier to see what to do than to understand verbal instructions in whatever language
  g) there is a rise in non-L1 speaking children in state and private school systems. The use of L1 to teach English will disadvantage their educational development.

- Students rarely learn what we think we are teaching them. Children absorb a lot of what they hear unconsciously. The more incidental language they hear around them, the more opportunities there are for them to pick it up in context.
- When sticking to an English-only policy, the primary teacher is sending the following messages to her students:
  - Languages are different.
  - You don't have to fear new languages.
  - You can understand.
  - You are under no pressure to use the new language...
  - ... but isn't it fun when you do?

E-mail: omadylus@hotmail.com

4.2 Foreign language corners

Sandie Mourão *Freelance, Portugal*

A foreign language (FL) corner is a space in a classroom which lets children interact freely with a foreign language. It allows for 'free play', child-initiated as opposed to teacher-directed activity. It also provides many opportunities for engaging with the foreign language as individuals, in pairs or in small groups.

Why is play so important for children and why should they be given opportunities to play with English?

- Play motivates!
- Play allows children to learn when they are ready, using each play experience in an individual way. (Moyles 1989: 23, 29)
- Play builds children's confidence in themselves and their abilities, so that physical and mental skills can be repeated again and again, providing confidence and mastery. (Moyles 1989: 23)
- Play 'provides for learning, without threat from things which go wrong' (Moyles 1989: 28).
- Play can be seen as a trial and error activity, with an emphasis on the non-serious. (Guha 1996: 62)
- Play is mediated by language, which leads to communal learning. (Wood & Attfield 1996: 68)

The Portuguese foreign language corner experience

In Portugal, the FL corner was set up by a group of twelve pre-school teachers. They used a selection of the following:

- FL games – often made with the children; simple flashcards, dominoes, bingo, board games, puzzles

- Visuals – posters or drawings that children have done, or postcards and pictures found in magazines
- Books and story cards – these included teacher-bought, teacher-made, class-made and parent-donated books and dictionaries
- Cassettes – recorded songs and rhymes, sometimes with portable headphones
- Puppets

Over a year, the FL corner changed and grew, accompanying the children's learning and interests. All the teachers involved are convinced of the appropriateness of such a corner and of its value for pre-school.

The children regularly chose the corner, and were able to play independently of their pre-school teacher, using the FL. Peer teaching was observed at all levels, children helped each other to remember key words or phrases, to pronounce words properly and even to get words in the right order. The FL corner successfully enabled the pre-school children to engage in using the FL.

The FL corner was not an easy thing to set up. It needed to be a dynamic space, where children had a choice of activities. However, no matter how much hard work the corner created, the positive results far outweighed the difficulties.

Setting up a play area for the FL could be the solution many teachers have been looking for in primary classrooms. Using the corner to provide free play in the FL not only offers children the opportunity to have fun with the language, try it out, gain confidence and help peers, but also very importantly, the corner naturally integrates the FL into the children's everyday school world.

4.3 ROLO: Reformulate Output Lightly but Often

Paul Emmerson *International House, England*

I have coined the term ROLO to describe the technique of doing language work diagnostically after tasks and skills practice.

Reformulate Output:

Start with students' real output (speaking or writing), then elicit/give more appropriate language as feedback in an extended slot at the end of the lesson.

Lightly:

Do this quickly, perhaps with a concept question, but without a heavy explanation.

Often:

Do this often, and revise the same points over several feedback slots.

Presentation–Practice lessons	ROLO lessons
Lesson begins with language work and moves on to skills practice.	Lesson begins with skills practice and moves on to language work in a feedback slot.
Language items are covered one at a time, in detail.	Many language items are covered in one feedback slot. Each item is covered lightly and often (i.e. in other feedback slots).
Language items are pre-selected, either from the pages of a coursebook or the lesson plan of a teacher.	Language items are not pre-selected: they arise naturally as a need/mistake during students' output in the lesson.
Focus on the presentation of new language. Appropriate for first contact between learner and language item.	Focus on activation of language students have already learned or been exposed to. Appropriate for all subsequent occasions when language item is needed or misused.
Appropriate as the main way of doing language work: • on extensive courses • where the backbone of the syllabus is the English verb tense system • where the students' objective is accuracy of form • where the students are studying to pass an exam	Appropriate as the main way of doing language work: • on short, intensive courses • where the backbone of the syllabus is topics and functional skills • where the students' objective is accuracy of meaning • where the students are studying to increase their ability to communicate effectively
Appropriate for large groups.	Appropriate for small groups. Absolutely essential for one-to-one.
Role of the teacher is classroom manager, managing the flow of language from off the pages of the coursebook or lesson materials to the students.	Role of the teacher is language consultant, managing the flow of language from the students back to the students. Requires T skill in choosing items for feedback.
Easier and safer for inexperienced teachers.	More interesting and fun for experienced teachers.
Acceptable and conventional for e.g. DELTA courses, BC inspections.	Questionable acceptability and very unusual for e.g. DELTA courses, BC inspections.

I described the mechanics of running a language feedback slot, including:

- Criteria for choosing items for feedback, e.g. trust your judgement ('If I had been a participant in this discussion, what would I have found difficult to understand?') and variety.
- The importance of silence after writing examples of language use on the board. This gives the students a chance to think about the example and activate their passive knowledge.
- Concept questions to activate and elicit knowledge if the students are stuck.

Finally, I gave suggestions for lesson plans using ROLO. Examples included summarizing a newspaper article, job word-maps and continuing discussions that started naturally in the coffee break.

E-mail: paulemmerson@lineone.net

4.4 Paralessons: What happens on the edge of lessons

Richard Kiely *University College Chichester, England*

This paper discusses the function of classroom discussions which take place between teacher and students before and after lessons, and during the break. The label 'paralessons' is used to signal two aspects of these interactions: they are both *parallel to*, and *beyond* the core lessons in terms of opportunities for learning and programme development. As an examination of the edge of a carpet reveals its design and weave, conversations on the edge of a programme facilitate a view of its construct, both in terms of the teacher's thinking and the students' experience.

Qualitative classroom data from an ethnographic study of an EAP programme in a British university are used to explore both the pedagogical and programme management functions of these interactions. These field notes and headnotes are augmented by data from interviews with the teacher and students, which provide insights into teacher and student perspectives on their purpose and value. The paper shows how these interactions demonstrate the social nature of classrooms, and how they are used to manage and develop the programme.

The data reveal four contexts of interaction in the break, two initiated by students, and two primarily teaching-related.

1 Students raise individual queries which they opted not to ask in the core lesson, or which are related to individual work. Examples include a query about a word explained by the teacher in the session but which was not clear to a student, how to criticize in essays, and information on assessment tasks.
2 Students clarify issues regarding the administration of the programme, particularly in relation to personal circumstances and commitments. Examples here include queries about the process for getting a certificate of attendance, and negotiation of the date of a presentation for assessment.
3 The teacher uses discussions with students in the break to assess their learning needs and suitability for the programme. Although this does not serve as a gateway to the programme – the students are centrally registered – it provides the teacher with insights into the needs of particular students, and may determine the kind of support which the teacher extends to students.
4 The one mandated interaction observed in the break is a brief tutorial on the topic of the assessed project. Here the teacher, over two weeks, speaks to all students about their choice of topic, and gives guidelines for focussing the oral presentation.

The phenomenon documented here has implications for three aspects of ELT. First, ELT programmes are peopled phenomena, with a network of relationships and interactions underpinning learning events and outcomes. Second, in relation to programme evaluation, good programmes are those which develop a strong network of relationships, rather than those which reflect more generalised, abstract criteria. Third, in relation to research, there is a need to explore the concepts evidenced by paralessons, such as the links between relationships, investment and motivation; classroom relationships and independent learning; and how teachers plan their use of interactions on the edge of lessons.

E-mail: R.Kiely@ucc.ac.uk

4.5 Dynamic drills and the generative principle

Wolfgang Butzkamm *Rheinisch-Westfälische Technische Hochschule, Germany*

The generative principle refers to the building of new forms according to known forms and applies to both word-formation and sentence-formation. This, of course, reminds us of pattern drills, which have often turned out to be mechanical and monotonous. Pattern practice, however, should not occur at the expense of communication, but should facilitate it. Therefore, the bilingual pattern drills which I propose here meet three different needs which are all important:

- the need to notice the pattern in a sentence, to see the slots into which different words may be plugged;
- the need to achieve fluency, to automatize a given sentence pattern (these two needs have been met by traditional pattern practice);
- the need to probe the communicative radius of a structure and explore its communicative potential. This is mainly achieved by focusing on the meanings of the sentence variations.

Initially, we use simple, easy substitutions. The focus is predominantly on form, i.e. on the first two needs. Any word will do which is easily accessible, fits the sentence pattern and makes sense. Later, we focus more and more on content.

Example: contact clause

Take, for instance, the line 'All I want is a room somewhere' from Eliza's song in the musical *My Fair Lady*. Initially, the teacher's idea is simply to practise the formal device of a 'contact clause' where the relative pronoun is left out. S/he explains the structure, which is unknown in German, by giving a literal translation:

All	I	want	is	a	room
Alles	*was ich*	*will*	*ist*	*ein*	*Zimmer*

The learner is now aware of the anatomy of the phrase. Then the teacher changes the German sentence to a more idiomatic phrase and starts out with easy substitutions, to achieve fluency:

Ich will ja nur eine Tasse Tee.
All I want is a cup of tea.
Ich will ja nur eine Tasse Kaffee.
All I want is a cup of coffee.
Ich will ja nur ein Glas Milch.
All I want is a glass of milk.
Sie will ja nur ein Glas Milch.
All she wants is a glass of milk.

If the teacher thinks the class needs further practice, s/he gives some more cues along the same lines. But then s/he changes the focus and starts to elicit the following sentence variations from the class, focusing on the things wanted:

Ich will ja nur eine ruhige Klasse.
All I want is a quiet class.
Ich will ja nur brave Schüler.
All I want is well-behaved pupils.
Ich will ja nur ein wenig Ruhe.
All I want is a little peace.
Sie will ja nur einen neuen Freund.
All she wants is a new boyfriend.

In the course of the exercise, we can change the tense and the verb as well:

Ich wollte ja nur einen Kuß.
All I wanted was a kiss.
Ich bekam nur ein freundliches Lächeln.
All I got was a friendly smile.

'Empty' sentences at the beginning, and at the end suggestive sentences powerful enough to conjure up certain situations. In the minds of the pupils, these are no longer grammatical permutations, but variations on the theme of wishes and dreams, rather than a structure drill.

This, however, is not yet the end of the exercise. In the third part, it is handed over to the pupils. They have now to make up their own sentences, and at this point the exercise becomes monolingual – the mother tongue drops away. By now, the pupils are well prepared to produce sentences – and ideas – of their own. Those few who have no ideas of their own are free to select any of the sentences that the teacher had cued before. The teacher might also allow the class a few minutes' silence to jot down any idea that comes to their minds. Most pupils will then produce sentences which are meaningful and relevant to them. This in turn will give the teacher the opportunity to ask the pupil a question and involve her/him in a brief communicative exchange before resuming the exercise.

Development and dynamics of the exercise

1 Teacher-directed, mother tongue cues for ignition. At the beginning, simple, easy sentences in rapid succession, finally more complex, 'loaded' sentences.
2 (optional, written) Short brainstorm to note down ideas. Perhaps meditative background music as used in Suggestopedia.[1]

3 Pupils produce sentences of their own. Teacher might intervene and ask questions concerning the ideas expressed by the pupils.
4 (optional, written) Pupils write small/short texts of their own, using the new structure at least once.

E-mail: Butzkamm@lfed.rwth-aachen.de

Note

[1] Editor's note: In the revised edition of *Techniques and Principles in Language Teaching* (Oxford University Press 2000), Diane Larsen-Freeman reports: 'Suggestopaedia is now called Desuggestopaedia to reflect the importance placed on desuggesting limitations on learning'

4.6 Focus on form in communicative classrooms

Helen Basturkmen *University of Auckland, New Zealand*

This talk reported on a study investigating interaction in communicative lessons, that is, lessons primarily oriented to exchanging messages. The study found that periodically, teachers and students took time out from exchanging messages to 'focus on form', i.e. to deal with issues of language form (grammar, pronunciation, discourse, etc.) that arose incidentally.

The data for the study comprised 12 hours of audio-recorded lessons from two lower intermediate classes of 12 students and their two native-speaker teachers of English in a private language school in Auckland, New Zealand. These were naturally occurring lessons described by their teachers as 'communicative' and involving activities, such as information gap, opinion gap, brainstorming, discussions of the meaning of reading passages, role plays, etc. The recordings were examined to identify instances when the participants took time out from the main discourse of exchanging messages to focus on the form of language items. These instances, termed 'focus on form episodes' were then examined in detail to establish:

- who instigated the focus on form episodes, teachers or students
- what types of language forms (grammar, vocabulary, discourse, pronunciation, etc.) were targeted
- whether focus on form arose from problems of understanding or not (i.e. negotiation of meaning or negotiation of form)

Findings showed that the communicative lessons offered students and teachers frequent opportunities to deal with language forms. 448 focus on form episodes were identified in the recorded lessons (a rate of one every 1.6 minutes). Students themselves were active in instigating focus on form (37% of episodes). The episodes mainly targeted vocabulary and to a slightly lesser extent, grammar, but few targeted discourse or pronunciation. We also found that 75% of the episodes constituted negotiation of form, rather than negotiation of meaning – in other words, classroom participants frequently took time out of their communicative activities to deal with questions and problems of language form, even though there was no actual problem of understanding.

The results of the study indicate that in the two classes we studied, communicative activities offered both teachers and students plentiful opportunities to work on linguistic accuracy within activities in instruction primarily oriented towards fostering language fluency. Such findings prompt us as language educators to reconsider the 'accuracy/fluency divide' and to consider how we may help learners benefit from the opportunities message-oriented activities can provide for focusing on form.

Following the talk, one participant from the audience asked whether any data had been collected from the 'communicative' type lessons of non-native speaker teachers of English. No such data had been collected, but it was suggested that this subject would make an interesting further study. Another participant suggested that probably not only the learner who initiates the focus on form episode learns from it, but also other students would benefit from overhearing the student–teacher or student–student interaction about language forms. A number of avenues for further research into 'focus on form' were discussed and suggestions made for how teachers might exploit such episodes.

E-mail: h.basturkmen@auckland.ac.nz

4.7 The Grammarbox

Elizabeth McMahon and Maria Heron *Bell Language School, England*

The grammatical syllabus of a coursebook often fails teachers and learners alike by not offering adequate opportunities for revision and recycling. Neither does it address the individual language needs of specific groups of learners. The 'Grammarbox' provides simple classroom activities, which allow the teacher and learners to revise language items and accommodate the specific grammatical needs of the learners.

It is a cheap, simple, low-tech classroom resource, which consists of a small, plastic compartmentalised box and a set of coloured index cards on which the activities are written. Ideally the cards should be categorised according to level (we used the same colour-coding system as used in our Study Centres) and can be either handwritten or typed. The activity cards and the corresponding answer cards should be numbered clearly, so that the students can record which they have used and an 'ongoing' index card should list the contents of the box.

The grammatical content of the 100 cards is mainly determined by:

- the coursebook syllabus
- the gaps in the syllabus
- individual student needs or wishes
- errors perceived by the teacher

The activities themselves are all quite short and simple in format and include:

- familiar exercise types such as those found in most grammar practice books
- grammar consciousness-raising activities which encourage the learners to talk about language use and use grammatical terminology
- information gap activities which promote oral interaction around a particular grammatical area

- gap-fill at both sentence and text level (where possible authentic texts have been used)
- dictations (gapped, dictogloss, etc.)

The cards can be used in several ways:

- Self-access: the students work through the cards, selecting the grammatical areas they need to work on. For this purpose the students need easy access to the box during and outside class time.
- Pair- and groupwork: for this purpose multiple copies of the cards are necessary.
- Full groupwork: when the teacher wants to revisit or clarify a specific grammatical area, the whole class can work on the same card.

This project was undertaken as classroom research over a period of about six months, working with small groups at various levels. We had very positive feedback from the learners when we gave them a written questionnaire. They appreciated the revision element of the cards and many were happy to re-do activities until they could complete them successfully. They also appreciated the fact that the cards were personalized, in that they reflected individual learner problems and also used names and situations which were familiar to them.

As teachers we found the cards successful in motivating the learners to become more aware of the gaps in their knowledge, more articulate about grammar and better able to use grammatical terminology. The cards can also be used as the constituent parts of whole-group quizzes or games and as fillers when the teacher needs to occupy individual students (especially in the context of larger multi-level classes where students complete activities at a different pace).

E-mail: liz.mcmahon@bell-schools.ac.uk
maria.heron@bell-schools.ac.uk

4.8 Benchmarks for oral assessment of tertiary level content-based Business English?

Richard J Alexander *Vienna University of Economics and Business Administration, Austria*

My presentation discussed tertiary level Business English (BE) courses. I addressed the very disparate and non-standardized BE assessment procedures and varying expectations of BE proficiency levels in Europe. I asked whether LCCI or UCLES BEC examinations can serve as benchmarks for the oral part of our syllabuses. I concluded that these examinations do not engage sufficiently with the requirements and expectations of content-based tertiary level BE courses where subject knowledge intertwines with language.

I pointed out some possible advantages for institutions which enter students for external examinations, but noted that the washback effect of examination schemes imported from outside can threaten autonomous syllabus design and curriculum planning. For such examinations neglect the role played by subject knowledge in assessing students' mastery over language in oral examinations. The fact is that specific purpose language ability (BE for students of business is such a case) results from the intertwining of specific topical and background knowledge with language abilities, often triggered by specific tasks or, in an academic setting, by examination formats testing specific subject-related cognitive skills.

Factoring in the 'business element' in BE requires careful thought. We need to be more aware of how close is the link between language ability and cognitive abilities of knowledge, comprehension, application, analysis, synthesis and evaluation in dealing with business subjects. The explicit connection with furthering transferable skills in tertiary level education was highlighted. Against this background, it is safe to assume that stakeholders with an interest in examinations in content-based, business-rich Business English will rightly expect 'more' than just a 'language' proficiency test. This 'worldly' element needs to be reflected more closely in our assessment practices. It should be part of our task as tertiary level Business English syllabus planners to help professional assessment and testing experts to take into consideration or even move towards the more 'worldly'.

In the ensuing lively discussion one questioner asked how both subject matter and BE abilities can be adequately assessed. Another person asked how closely the subject specialists in tertiary education need to be involved in BE syllabuses. Some scepticism was expressed as to whether the BE teacher's job was to address business topics. Several participants raised the perennially controversial issue of how much subject knowledge BE teachers need to have. In the eyes of some participants, the professional development of teachers, especially in tertiary education, needed to contain some training in business. Others claimed that the BE teacher ought to have a double qualification: in EFL and in business studies. As presenter, I was fascinated to realize that I had touched a nerve which appeared to be common to many institutions outside my own in Austria. This shows that the issue of benchmarking should perhaps not be left to external examining bodies. Those of us involved tertiary level BE teaching need to be more proactive in our work. Real demand is so diffuse that we as professionals do well to reclaim our role in influencing the BE 'market' from the supply-side of the process.

E-mail: richard.alexander@wu-wien.ac.at

5 THE FUTURE OF GLOBAL ENGLISH: The Guardian Weekly/Macmillan Heinemann debate

Principles and policies for a multilingual Europe

Robert Phillipson

English permeates globalisation, Europeanisation and Americanisation. EU language policy is, apart from some rights to interpretation in the supra-national institutions, and the promulgation of documents in all official languages (which in theory have equal rights), largely covert. This facilitates the dominance of English. In several member states the impact of English has led to an awareness that local values are at risk: strategies for increased multilingualism aim at appropriating English without being victimised by it. Robert Phillipson argues that the European Union's bid to create unity will remain an ideal without a better policy on languages.

English yes, but equal language rights first

The 11 official languages of the 15 member states of the European Union have equal rights. These languages are Danish, Dutch, English, Finnish, French, German, Greek, Italian, Portuguese, Spanish and Swedish. The languages of each member state are official and working languages of the European Parliament and the Commission in Brussels.

Since there has never been a close fit between language and state in Europe, three of Belgium's languages are in use, Dutch, French and German, and two of Finland's, Finnish and Swedish, whereas the only language from Spain is Spanish, even though there are more speakers of Catalan than of Danish or Finnish. Demography is less important than political clout, nationally and internationally. Many languages in Europe have no EU rights.

EU languages permeate the ongoing processes of creating a 'union' of EU states, a new supra-national economic and political entity. Language is a sensitive political issue, as it is a profound symbol of national and personal identity. As language, culture and education are in principle matters for individual member states rather than the Union, language policy at the supra-national level is largely implicit and covert. As some languages are more 'international' than others, the equality of the 11 languages has in fact always been a myth.

The existing rights to translation are essential, because documents emanating from Brussels have the force of law in member states, overriding national legislation. The right to an interpreter is often restricted, except for senior politicians and Members of the European Parliament. Working documents are seldom available in all 11 languages. In 1970, 60% of texts in the Commission were initially drafted in French, and 40% in German. In 1989 the figures were French 50%, German 9%, and English 30%. By 1997 the figures were French 40% and English 45%, leaving only a sprinkling in other languages. In external communication, English is generally used. These figures reveal the *de facto* hierarchy of languages in Brussels and Strasbourg. English has gradually eroded the monopoly of French. Ironically enough, this has happened during a period when successive British governments have kept 'Europe' at arm's length. The language policies of EU institutions are influenced by many factors, the most important of which is globalisation. The advance of English reflects American commercial, political and military might, and the impact of Hollywood, CNN and McDonald's.

The British have always been keen to capitalise on English as a strategic and commercial asset. English is the most widely learned foreign language in Europe, because Britain's partners recognise it as a necessary communicative tool. In reality English is no longer a foreign language in several member states. It is widely used internally in many fields, and increasingly as the corporate language of big business. It is a fact of working and social life for many EU citizens.

The market forces that are propelling English forward impact on the vitality and viability of other languages. English is capturing some of their territory, despite EU treaties and summit meetings proclaiming a commitment to diversity. The Amsterdam Treaty, Article 128.4 reads: 'The Community shall take cultural aspects into account in its action under the provisions of this Treaty, in particular in order to respect and to promote the diversity of its cultures.' The Nice summit acted on this to approve a programme to strengthen the European film industry.

In several member states there are voices protesting against Americanisation and cultural and linguistic homogenisation. Ulrich Ammon has recently written a book exploring whether German, the leading language of the natural sciences a century ago, can still be considered a language of science.

The Norwegian Minister of Transport has protested about the website of the SAS airline, which has the three Scandinavian governments as majority shareholders, being exclusively in English. The Swedish government recently commissioned a major survey of Swedish in all key domains in Sweden and in European Union institutions. The study documents how English is taking over from Swedish. Work is now under way to ensure that Swedish remains a 'complete' language. Investigations of domain loss to English in all the Nordic languages are currently being commissioned.

Several countries are thus following in the steps of the French in registering that the advance of English is a problem, and identifying strategies to strengthen local languages. No one is suggesting that English should not be effectively learned and used, but policy should ensure that people learn and use English in addition to other languages rather than at their expense.

Language policy ought to be taken seriously because it is likely that big business is doing so. A recent doctoral study in international law in the United States concludes that French language protection measures are in conflict with the principle of a common market with free movement of goods, services, labour and capital. Such an interpretation could soon lead corporate lawyers to challenge national language legislation, and demand an English-only market throughout the EU.

Countries applying for EU membership have probably assumed that their languages will have the same rights as other official languages. This is most unlikely, since the present interpretation and translation services are ineffective, and will be even more unworkable when new states join the EU. There needs to be a re-think of attitudes. Scoffing at French efforts to shore up French is myopic. If native speakers of French and English can use their mother tongues, how can one ensure equivalent rights for others?

What is urgently needed is clarification of the criteria that should guide an equitable language policy, and mechanisms that permit real equality of communication between speakers of different languages. We need imaginative and realistic scenarios. We need to see a coming together of the relevant constituencies in the political, business, academic, cultural and human rights worlds. There is a need for hard-nosed analysis of how to ensure efficient, cost-effective and democratic strategies for increased multilingualism. In this way English can be appropriated without other languages being marginalised.

Reference

Ammon U (2001) The Dominance of English as a Language of Science: Effects on Other Languages and Language Communities. Berlin: Mouton de Gruyer

Robert Phillipson

Robert Phillipson is currently Research Professor at the Department of English, Copenhagen Business School. He is the author of *Linguistic Imperialism* (OUP 1992), and his latest publication, as editor, *Rights To Language: Equity, Power And Education* (Lawrence Erlbaum Associates 2000) highlights his concern with language rights, globalisation and English, and language policy in the European Union. He has lectured world-wide and is a board member of the Danish Centre for Human Rights. He is British.

English as a lingua franca for Europe

Juliane House

The role of English as a worldwide lingua franca is irreversible. It is therefore more fruitful to accept this role than either to bemoan it or to follow the European Union's hypocritical language policy. A distinction between a 'language for communication' and a 'language for identification' is useful here. English as a lingua franca (ELF) is a language for communication, and as such the 'property' of all European speakers whose native languages will continue to serve as languages for identification, i.e., means for speakers to identify with their linguistic community's cultural heritage. The usefulness of this 'division of labour' is reflected in three recent developments: a renewed concern with local, regional and national linguistic and cultural practices; attempts to give English as a school subject a curricular status markedly different from other foreign languages; results from empirical research into ELF interactions and the influence of ELF on discourse norms in other European languages.

A stateless language that Europe must embrace

The language policy in the European Union is both ineffective and hypocritical, and its ideas of linguistic equality and multilingualism are costly and cumbersome illusions. Why have these illusions been kept up for so long? First, because the French, with their traditionally superior position in Europe, cannot accept the decline of their own linguistic power; second, because the politically correct ideologies of some sociolinguists constantly fuel opposition against the idea of English as a European lingua franca; and third, because powerful translators' lobbies fight for their raison d'être. In the name of the high ideal of linguistic equality, a time-consuming, expensive and increasingly intractable translation machinery is maintained that is doing its best to translate the illusion of equality into illusions of multilingualism and translatability.

The translations produced in the world's largest translation bureau are taken as tokens for equality: what counts is that they exist, not what they are like – many EU officials doubt their accuracy and openly prefer to read the more reliable English and French originals. Also, the supposed linguistic equality in the EU is a relative one: some languages are clearly more equal than others, and minority languages inside the member states do not count at all.

The EU's ostensible multilingualism sets it apart from other international organisations. Instead of having opted for a 'workable' number of working languages, all the official languages of the member states have been given equal status. For a smooth functioning of the EU institutions, however, whose legislation ordinary people do not understand anyway, the use of English as a lingua franca would be infinitely better.

English is particularly suitable as Europe's lingua franca because of its functional flexibility and spread across the world, and because English is already 'de-nativised' to a large extent: the global number of non-native speakers is now substantially larger than its native speakers (about 4:1). English is no longer 'owned' by its native speakers because acculturation and nativisation processes have produced a remarkable diversification of the English language into many non-native varieties.

The point is that we can no longer say that English is one monolithic, 'hegemonic' voice – it is a diversity of different voices. True, there may still be attempts by 'inner circle' English native speakers to perpetuate old dichotomies of 'us and them', of one-way translation avenues, of controlling access to professional organisations and publications. But this has nothing to do with the English language itself, which is neutral. Such imbalance simply reflects unequal power resulting from differences in social, economic, political or scientific conditions.

The multiplicity of voices behind English as a lingua franca implies that differences in interactional norms between speakers using English as a language for communication remain unaltered. And it is this deep diversity in the use of English by speakers with different mother tongues which invalidates the claim that English is an imperialist adversary, an eliminating 'killer language' – which English, we may ask?

Is it those localised, regionalised or otherwise appropriated varieties of English whose speakers creatively conduct pragmatic and cultural shifts? Surely not. Arguments such as the ones brought forward by the anti-English league are simply outdated. The Empire has struck back already. Non-native speakers of English have created their own discourse norms and genres. And they do this of their own free will, happily ignoring the 'linguistic domination' ascribed to them. In other words, there is no didactic-linguistic replay of formerly colonial and militaristic means.

But might not the use of English also change other European languages to the point of gradually destroying their identities? Is English maybe already 'colonising' structural and discourse conventions in other European languages? Not at all. Research funded by the German Research Foundation has shown that German, Spanish and French texts resulting from multilingual text production are not influenced by the English language on these levels. And another research project, investigating the nature of interactions in English between speakers of different European languages, has revealed differences in culture conditioned ways of interacting, which, however, do not lead to misunderstanding.

English as a lingua franca is nothing more than a useful tool: it is a 'language for communication', a medium that is given substance with the different national, regional, local and individual cultural identities its speakers bring to it. English itself does not carry such identities, it is not a 'language for identification'. And because of the variety of functional uses of global English, English also has a great potential for promoting international understanding. Its different speakers must always work out a common behavioural and intercultural basis.

Paradoxical as this may seem, the very spread of English can motivate speakers of other languages to insist on their own local language for identification, for binding them emotionally to their own cultural and historical tradition. There is no need to set up an old-fashioned dichotomy between local languages and English as the 'hegemonic aggressor': there is a place for both, because they fulfil different functions. To deny this is to uphold outdated concepts of monolingual societies and individuals. German speakers, for instance, keep their national language and regional varieties for identification while simultaneously benefiting from using English to establish 'imagined communities'[1] in science, economics, etc. for pockets of expertise.

In western Germany in particular, English has been widely accepted as a language for communication since 1945 – not least because the Anglo-Saxon countries served as models of democracy helping people to forget their own past. And a recent survey of German teachers' attitudes to English revealed unanimous support for using English as a lingua franca in Europe; no one thought English destroyed the identity of their mother tongues; no one felt that communicating in English led to inequality between speakers of English and speakers of different languages.

Using English as a lingua franca in Europe does not inhibit linguistic diversity, and it unites more than it divides, simply because it may be 'owned' by all Europeans – not as a cultural symbol, but a means of enabling understanding.

Note

[1] Editor's note: see Benedict Anderson *Imagined Communities* Verso 1983; revised and extended 1991

Juliane House

Juliane House was educated at the Universities of Heidelberg and Toronto. She is professor of Applied Linguistics and head of the English language programme at the University of Hamburg. Her main research interests are in the areas of contrastive and interlanguage pragmatics, translation theory and intercultural communication and misunderstanding. She is currently researching the nature of interactions in English as a lingua franca, and the influence English may have on discourse norms in other European languages via translation and multilingual text production.

Can minority languages survive?

John Walsh

Because of the frequent threats to their existence, research into many autochthonous minority language communities provides valuable insights into the links between language, identity and self-esteem. Minority language organisations throughout the EU are now trying to further develop this link, and to use identity and positive self-worth as a motor for their communities' socio-economic development. New technologies and new media are being explored as means of overcoming geographical and economic marginalisation, based on the link between identity and linguistic specificity. Bilingual or trilingual education projects are being pursued, in order to give the native language equal status in schools with English and other dominant languages. The increasing presence in Europe of 'new' minorities, represented by refugees and asylum-seekers, will henceforth pose new challenges both to autochthonous linguistic minorities and national and regional governments, particularly in the fields of education and media policy.

Minority voices show strong instinct for survival

The debate about dominant and dominated languages in Europe concentrates almost exclusively on the position of English versus the ten other official languages. Yet the simplistic claim that English – the 'international shark' as one commentator has dramatically called it – is about to devour other state languages, ignores a far more diverse tapestry of linguistic diversity. According to the Brussels-based European Bureau for Lesser Used Languages, about 40m people in Europe speak a language other than the dominant language of the country where they reside. These languages range in strength from the Catalan pike, with about 7m speakers, to the minnow of Saterfrisian, a minority language in Germany spoken by about 2,000 people. In between are more than 60 other language minorities, each finding itself in entirely different circumstances and faced with its own specific predator.

Basques in the south of France are concerned at the continuing refusal of the French government to grant their language adequate protection in education and the media. An island in a sea of Dutch, Frisians have been shocked by a recent study revealing poor standards of teaching their languages in schools. Slovenes in the southern Austrian province of Carinthia are alarmed at government cutbacks which threaten to close bilingual Slovene-German radio stations. In the Italian minority region of Slovenia, the Italian parts of bilingual roadsigns were recently painted over. No one replaced Italian with English. English is not the main concern of these minorities.

Yet despite these examples, it is not the case that all minority languages across Europe are being swallowed up by their own national sharks. The recent establishment of a private bilingual Breton-French television station was a kick in the teeth to those on the French right who have fought, as far as constitutional level, against recognition of minority languages in France. Linguistic minorities in Italy have had a good year, with far-reaching national legislation allowing them to finally begin consolidating their education and media. Protection of minorities in the Danish-German border region is conducted on the basis of international reciprocal agreements between both countries. And the European Bureau for Lesser Used Languages brings together representatives of all minorities three times a year to exchange experiences and to press the EU for funding and recognition.

This does not mean, however, that minority language communities are ignorant about the dominance of English, oblivious to anything other than their own regional struggles. Notwithstanding their problems with education, the Frisians last year began a pilot project dividing primary school hours between their own language, Dutch and English. A similar project was recently launched in the Basque Country with equal emphasis on Basque, Spanish and English. And in Luxembourg, English is indeed the first foreign language taught to schoolchildren, but not before they master Luxemburgish, French and German.

This latter point is worth making because it underlines another important element of the dynamic. Speakers of minority languages cannot afford to be against learning the dominant language surrounding them. They have no choice in the matter, as this language is essential for communication with their neighbours, sometimes literally in the next house.

This does not mean, however, that they should discard their native language as if it were an impediment to progress. It is true that this has happened, dramatically in the case of Ireland, and still continues to happen in some of the smaller minorities. But acquisition of English or any other dominant language does not have to occur at the expense of the language of the home or community.

Most theorists agree that language remains the primary marker of identity. The slow yet perceptible development of academic theories exploring the links between identity, language and socio-economic development is becoming another important support mechanism for minority language communities. The Brussels-based Research Centre on Multilingualism has recently urged the development of 'econolinguistics', a new academic discipline linking multilingualism and economic development.

The Centre's research could also point towards ways of developing an equitable language policy at EU level. It suggests the development of a language policy based on the same compensatory principles already used in agricultural and regional economic policies. This would form the basis of an EU programme for all languages with limited geographical bases or facing other threats to their future vitality (which could, of course, include 'smaller' languages such as Danish or Finnish).

The central planks of such a programme would be: positive discrimination, such as providing financial support for producing materials or training personnel in the language; decentralisation, to allow enhanced use of the language at local level; and the overall promotion of multilingualism where no language is developed at the expense of another. Such a suggestion could help overcome the current narrow debate about the future of official languages in an enlarged Union.

Finally, an issue which is increasingly gaining attention in the language debate, but with which EU leaders are showing little enthusiasm to engage: the languages of immigrant communities. Most of the discourse about lesser-used languages focuses solely on indigenous or autochthonous minorities, referred to in some states as 'national minorities'. In a country such as Germany, where Turks far outnumber any indigenous language group, the issue of immigrant community languages can no longer be ignored.

Quite apart from the fact that the 'new' immigrant communities will be the 'old' minorities of tomorrow, their languages often face similar, if not more acute problems than 'national' groups. In the Netherlands, itself containing a high percentage of immigrants, research has begun into the common challenges facing both 'old' and 'new'.

Whether or not the EU is willing to include the thorny issue of immigration in a future language policy remains a point of debate, but neither 'old' nor 'new' are displaying any willingness to be consumed by the international shark of English.

John Walsh

John Walsh was Editor of Eurolang, the Brussels-based news agency dealing with minority language issues. He studied Celtic languages at University College Dublin before working for six years as a journalist with RTE, the Irish state broadcaster, and the Irish language television channel, TG4. He is currently carrying out research work at Dublin City University, where he is undertaking a PhD in minority languages and socio-economic development. He speaks Irish, English, Welsh, French and Dutch.

Teaching English as a lingua franca for Europe

Barbara Seidlhofer

Computational corpus linguistics, the analysis of vast amounts of electronically stored written and spoken text, has had a powerful impact on mainstream English language teaching, in which the predominant model (still) is 'native' English. I will explore the relevance of current corpus research for the description and teaching of English as a lingua franca, the most widespread use of English in Europe and worldwide. I will go on to discuss the potentially radical ways in which our curricula, teaching materials and teacher education may change when the implications of the global spread of English and new technologies for linguistic description are carried through to pedagogy.

Accents of English in Europe

Jennifer Jenkins

Given that there are now more second language than first language speakers of English around the globe, dramatic developments in spoken English are likely to occur over the coming years. In Europe, we may be about to witness the emergence of a hybrid European accent, albeit with local variations, which will no longer look to Britain to dictate its norms or 'police' its use. I will explore the concept of a European English accent and relate it to my proposals for a 'lingua franca pronunciation core' for English when it is spoken internationally.

Bringing Europe's lingua franca into the classroom

A Finnish scientist coming to Vienna for a conference on human genetics; an Italian designer negotiating with prospective clients in Stockholm; a Polish tourist chatting with local restaurateurs in Crete: they all communicate successfully in 'English', but which 'English'? Well, chances are that it is not the language you hear in chat shows and soaps on British or American television, but rather a range of 'Englishes', with enough of a common core so as to make it viable as a means of communication.

In fact, it is even claimed that a European variety of English, sometimes labelled 'Euro-English', is in the process of evolving to serve as a European lingua franca. As yet, however, this new variety of English has not been described, largely because it is at such an embryonic stage in its evolution. All we can say with any degree of certainty is that English as a lingua franca in Europe (ELFE) is likely to be some kind of European-English hybrid which, as it develops, will increasingly look to continental Europe rather than to Britain or the United States for its norms of correctness and appropriateness.

However, as long as there is no sound empirical basis for a description of how the language is actually used, the forms ELFE will take will remain an object of speculation.

This is why we decided to record interactions among 'non-native' speakers of English from a wide variety of first-language backgrounds, and to investigate what happens linguistically when English is used as a lingua franca. The focus of our research to date has been on pronunciation and lexicogrammar (vocabulary plus grammar), and it has enabled us to make a number of educated guesses at emerging characteristics of ELFE.

Jennifer Jenkins gathered data from interactions among non-native speakers of English in order to establish which aspects of pronunciation cause intelligibility problems when English is spoken as an international language. This enabled her to draw up a pronunciation core, the Lingua Franca Core, and certain of the features she designates core and non-core provide evidence as to the likely development of ELFE pronunciation.

The features of the Lingua Franca Core are those which were found to be crucial for intelligibility. They include:

- consonant sounds except for *th* (both voiceless as in *think* and voiced as in *this*) and dark *l* (as, for example, in the word *hotel*)
- vowel length contrasts (e.g. the difference in length between the vowel sounds in the words *live* and *leave*)
- nuclear (tonic) stress (e.g. the stress indicated by capital letters in the following: 'I come from FRANCE. Where are YOU from?')

Most other areas of pronunciation are then designated non-core, and these include many features on which teachers and learners often spend a great deal of time and effort, such as the exact quality of vowel sounds, word stress, or the 'typical rhythm of British English', with lots of 'little' words such as articles and prepositions pronounced so weakly as to be hardly audible.

Taking the Lingua Franca Core as our starting point, we predict that the pronunciation of ELFE will, over time, develop certain characteristics. For example, it is unlikely that *th* will be a feature of ELFE accents since nearly all continental Europeans other than those from Spain and Greece have a problem in producing it. What is not clear at this stage is whether the ELFE substitute will be *s* and *z* (as used, for example, by many French- and German-English speakers) or *t* and *d* (as used, for example, by many Italian- and Scandinavian-English speakers), or whether there will be scope for regional variation. Given that users of *s* and *z* outnumber users of *t* and *d*, however, we predict that ultimately the former will become the accepted ELFE variant. Similarly, because of difficulties of many Europeans with dark *l*, we predict that this sound will not be included in the ELFE pronunciation inventory, but will probably be substituted with clear *l* (a development which will run counter to that in British English, where dark *l* is increasingly being substituted with l-vocalisation, such that *bill* sounds more like 'biw').

On the other hand, we predict that the British English distinction between voiced and voiceless consonants is likely to be maintained in ELFE, since the loss of this distinction proved to be a frequent cause of intelligibility problems in the research. For example, a German-English speaker's devoicing of the final sound on the word *mug* so that it sounded like 'muck' rendered the word unintelligible to an Italian-English speaker.

The phenomena which can be observed in the area of ELFE lexicogrammar are the research focus of Barbara Seidlhofer's current work. For this purpose, she has been compiling a corpus of interactions in English among fairly fluent speakers from a variety of first-language backgrounds. This corpus, supported by Oxford University Press, is called the Vienna-Oxford ELF Corpus and is housed at the University of Vienna.

The findings emerging from it are similar to Jenkins' research into pronunciation in that they also involve many of those features often regarded, and taught, as particularly 'typical' of (native) English. In our analyses of a variety of interactions such as casual conversations and academic discussions, no major disruptions in communication occurred when speakers committed one or more of the following deadly grammatical 'sins':

- using the same form for all present tense verbs, as in 'You look very sad' and 'He look very sad'
- not putting a definite or indefinite article in front of nouns, as in 'Our countries have signed agreement about this'
- treating *who* and *which* as interchangeable relative pronouns, as in 'the picture who...' or 'a person which...'
- using just the verb stem in constructions such as 'I look forward to see you tomorrow'
- using *isn't it*? as a universal tag question (i.e. instead of *haven't they*? and *shouldn't he*?), as in 'They've finished their dinner now, isn't it?'

These characteristics, it will be noted, are described in a neutral way here, i.e. we are not talking about 'dropping the third person *-s*' or 'leaving out the *-ing* ending of the gerund', but this is not the way these 'mistakes' are usually treated in English classrooms around Europe. As many teachers of English as a foreign language will know, the time and effort spent on such features as the 'third person *-s*', the use of articles and the 'gerund' is often considerable, and nevertheless many learners still fail to use them 'correctly' after years of instruction, especially in spontaneous speech.

What our analyses of ELF interactions suggest is that the time needed to teach and learn these constructions bears very little relationship to their actual usefulness, as successful communication is obviously possible without them. It seems, in fact, that there is a very good reason for many students' observed resistance to learning these characteristics of native-speaker English: like the *th-* sounds discussed above, they are not communicatively crucial. Rather, speakers tend to tune into them only when they use English in a native-speaker community and wish to 'blend in' (which, for certain learners, obviously remains a desirable objective) while they seem to be redundant in much lingua franca communication.

As far as the implications for teaching are concerned, we would like to make two general suggestions. The first and most important point to emphasise is, in our view, the need to encourage both teachers and students to adjust their attitudes towards ELFE. Even those who strongly support the development of a continental European hybrid variety of English that does not look to Britain or America for its standards of correctness, reveal a degree of schizophrenia in this respect. For example, Charlotte Hoffman has described the English of European learners as spanning 'the whole range from non-fluent to native-like', as though fluency in English were not a possibility for those whose speech does not mimic that of a native speaker.

Similarly, Theo van Els pointed out in a lecture given last year in the Netherlands that the ownership of a lingua franca transfers from its native speakers to its non-native speakers. Yet he went on to argue paradoxically that the Dutch should not be complacent about their English because 'only very few are able to achieve a level of proficiency that approximates the native or native-like level'.

Our second point is that it is crucial for English language teaching in Europe to focus on contexts of use that are relevant to European speakers of English. In particular, descriptions of spoken English offered to these learners should not be grounded in British or American uses of English but in ELFE or other non-native contexts (depending on where the particular learners intend to use their English in future).

In this respect it is disappointing that so-called 'authentic' materials offered to learners continue to be based only on corpora of native speaker use. For example, Helen Basturkmen's recent contribution to the *ELT Journal* (2001: 12) argues in favour of 'highlighting general strategies of talk, and encouraging learners to become active observers of language use in settings relevant to them'. This would be admirable were it not the conclusion to an article in which she cites examples taken exclusively from data of native speaker interactions. ELFE learners (along with all other learners of English as an International Language) need descriptions drawn from interactions between non-native speakers in the contexts in which they, too, will later participate. To some, our proposal may seem to be a recipe for 'permissiveness' and a decline in 'standards'. But what we are essentially seeking to do is to carry through the implications of the fact that English *is* an international language and as such no longer the exclusive preserve of its native speakers. If English is indeed a lingua franca, then it should be possible to describe it as such without prejudice. And that may well be the biggest challenge for ELFE in the twenty-first century.

Reference

Helen Basturkmen (2001) Descriptions of spoken language for higher level learners: the example of questioning. In *ELT Journal* Vol 55/1

Barbara Seidlhofer

Barbara Seidlhofer is Associate Professor at the English Department of Vienna University. Her principal interest is in applied linguistics for language teacher education, especially the relationship between language description and pedagogic practice. Her publications include *Pronunciation* (with C Dalton, OUP 1994), *Principle and Practice in Applied Linguistics* (co-edited with G Cook, OUP 1995), and *Language Policy and Language Education in Emerging Nations* (co-editor, Ablex 1998). She is currently working on a book on the description and pedagogy of English as a lingua franca.

Jennifer Jenkins

Dr Jennifer Jenkins is co-ordinator of Teacher Education and Applied Linguistics in the English Language Centre, King's College London. She has carried out extensive research on English pronunciation within an international framework, her latest and most controversial publication being *The Phonology Of English As An International Language* (OUP 2000).

6 FOCUS ON THE LEARNER

6.1 Aptitude in foreign language learning

Richard Masterson *University College, Cork, Ireland*

This workshop considered contrasting teacher and learner perspectives on foreign and second language learning aptitude. Reference was made to Carroll's (1962) descriptors for the four abilities he recognized as comprising language learning aptitude: phonetic coding, grammatical sensitivity, rote learning ability and inductive learning ability, as well as Stansfield's (1991) description of general learning aptitude as 'the amount of time it takes an individual to learn a task in question', and insights into aptitude by Skehan (1989), Sternberg et al (2001), Reynolds (2001) and Mclaughlin (1995), amongst others.

Data was presented based on responses to two different questionnaires given to teachers and students in order to elicit views of foreign language learning strengths and weaknesses of particular students. Teachers at the Language Centre, University College, Cork were asked to use the Carroll descriptors as a point of reference in identifying what they perceived as relatively high and relatively low aptitude for learning EFL. Those students identified were then interviewed on the basis of a questionnaire asking about their EFL learning and indirectly including the abilities identified by Carroll. In the interviews, students were also taught specific grammatical and vocabulary items in order to investigate their pace of uptake in a non-threatening environment.

Participants at the workshop were asked in groups to consider case studies of particular students, based on printed data relating to one student, perceived by their teachers to have relatively high EFL learning aptitude, and another perceived to have relatively low aptitude (one of each for each group of workshop participants). From the data based on learner interviews, participants were asked to compare the two learners and to consider:

- how they would deal with the student with apparently lower aptitude in class and in training outside the class
- what significant information about the student was missing from the interview notes
- what else they needed to know about the learner in order to help him or her to become a more effective EFL learner

Participants in groups then presented points from their deliberations and a number of interesting issues were presented and discussed, e.g.:

- radical differences in teacher and learner and workshop participants' perception of EFL learning aptitude
- the difficulty of disentangling aptitude from learner motivation, learner styles, the effects of educational experience and so on
- the issue of teachers' understanding of problems emanating from the learners' first language
- the difficulty of distinguishing, for example, oral fluency from an understanding of pronunciation patterns in English and difficulties in inferring possible pronunciation of sounds and words
- the difficulty of relating spelling patterns to pronunciation patterns in English

Some concerns were expressed about the difficulty of eliciting students' views of their own foreign language learning aptitude in such a two-way teacher/student study, as well as the relative reliability of teacher and student judgements. In the study, I had in fact asked students what they felt to be their strengths and weaknesses as EFL learners, while at the same time investigating their learning in the actual interviews as a point of comparison with the teacher data already presented to workshop participants. The main purpose of the workshop was an awareness-raising exercise aimed at developing more effective teacher learning and a greater understanding between learners and teachers. In e-mails sent to me since the session, participants from different countries and different teaching environments have expressed considerable interest in the area of second language learning aptitude.

E-mail: rmasterson@langcent.ucc.ie

6.2 Learning strategies: A case in autonomy

Iphigenia Mahili *Technological Educational Institute, Greece*

How ready are our students to become autonomous learners? Can strategy training lead to better strategy use? This talk addressed these questions by describing and discussing a comparative study of two groups of technical English college students, who received different kinds of strategy training – one (A) totally autonomous and the other (B) 'gradually autonomous'. The purpose of the study was to see the effect of strategy training on the students' vocabulary and reading skills, the differences – if any – in strategies pre- and post-course, and finally to determine which of the two methods of training was the more effective.

In Group A, autonomy was fostered from the very beginning without any previous training. Instead of classroom instruction, students engaged in periodic personal goal-setting, decision-making about course content and materials, monthly peer- and self-assessment and justification for these decisions in weekly meetings with the teacher. The training they received was uninformed and minimal. In Group B, on the other hand, autonomy was initiated by degrees, starting with consciousness raising, gradually training them to take responsibility for their progress and finally engage in full self-evaluation. Training materials for both groups included a packet of technical reading passages and a booklet with information on learning strategies.

Pre- and post-course tests on vocabulary and reading were administered to measure and compare learner outcomes – to see whether the students had acquired the technical vocabulary studied and improved their reading of passages in their discipline. Also, an inventory was administered at the beginning and at the end of the course to determine differences in strategy use. Finally, changes in student beliefs about language learning, autonomy, motivation and personal abilities were determined through an attitude questionnaire given before and after training. Comparisons were made pre- and post-course and between groups.

Results showed clear differences between the two groups. The trained group performed much better in the tests, though more in vocabulary than in reading, and showed a greater change in overall strategy use than the other group. Findings from the attitude questionnaire correlated with those concerning performance and strategy use. Since the study was conducted in a mixed ability class with students from highly diverse backgrounds, an analysis of numerous factors (such as level, motivation and background in English) was carried out and correlated with strategy use. The findings revealed that choice of strategies is highly dependent on the character and individual preferences of each learner and concluded that it is important to respect that and to encourage our students to find what suits them best. The initial hypothesis about autonomy was confirmed: autonomy can be achieved, but after training the learners how to think, how to make choices and how to substantiate their decisions.

At the end of the talk, the presenter addressed questions about the methodology used, exceptional cases noticed and the learners' overall attitude toward the study. Interest was expressed in obtaining more details on the results, and experiences and opinions were shared about the effectiveness of autonomy and strategy training.

E-mail: ifigenia@otenet.gr

6.3 Self-directed learning: The interaction between internal and external factors

Maria de los Angeles Clemente *Universidad Autonoma de Oaxaca, Mexico*

Even a brief glance at the research into autonomy over the past 20 years is enough to indicate the stress that has been given to the *self*, believing that the role of internal factors (such as *self-knowledge*, *self-analysis* and *self-correction* to name a few) is far more important than that of external factors (such as having a teacher as decision-maker or as a provider of feedback). Moreover, this approach implies a dependence/independence dichotomy, which assumes that independence is in every respect desirable, and that dependence is a state to be avoided. With this kind of approach (e.g. Sheerin in Benson & Voller (Ed.), *Autonomy and Independence in Language Learning*, Longman 1997), the field of learner autonomy runs the risk of appearing not to tolerate diversity because it rejects those learners who opt for a more other-directed approach to learning languages..

To illustrate the role and interaction of internal and external factors, the presentation included data (from language learners in a self-access centre in Mexico) about the way learners focus their attention on specific elements of the target language. The interpretation of this data suggests that in order to make a decision regarding what to focus on, learners assess the situation according to a variety of factors, both internal and external. Internal factors included an awareness of their personal histories as language learners (including past failures), their specific needs, styles and priorities, and their lack of readiness or knowledge. Among the external factors mentioned were textbook instructions, exercises and transcriptions, as well as human resources (teachers, counsellors).

What is important here is not simply the constant presence of both internal and external factors, but the fact that the two are interdependent. The data suggests that it is wrong to think that the reference to external factors means that the learner is not autonomous and able to make critical decisions about his/her learning processes. It also shows that very 'independent' and assertive learners still take advantage of external resources, such as the teacher or the instructions in a textbook. In my view, autonomy (see Clemente in Little, Dam and Timmer, *Focus on learning rather than teaching: why and how?* Dublin, Trinity College 2000) is a critical state of engagement and awareness that allows the learner to make informed decisions, even if this means following the directions of a teacher.

There are implications here both for our conception of the role of the self-directed learning counsellor and also for the role of classroom learners. I would argue that language learners can manage their own learning more effectively if they become more aware of how the external and internal factors work in alliance. Of course many teachers involved in self-directed programmes are already well aware of the connection between internal and external factors (as one member of the audience pointed out). My interest, then, is in developing a theoretical framework which provides a supporting theoretical rationale.

E-mail: angelesclemente@hotmail.com

6.4 Guessing it right: Successful strategies in vocabulary comprehension

Luis Guerra and Paulo Mendes *University of Évora, Portugal*

Successful reading does not solely depend on vocabulary comprehension. There are a number of other relevant skills activated in the process of understanding a text. Nevertheless, vocabulary knowledge enhances effective text comprehension more than any other component of reading.

In order to help learners cope with vocabulary problems, teachers should provide them with a range of strategies. The aim of our study was to analyze the strategies used by learners who try to discover the meaning of a new word by themselves. Since we only made use of a written text and in order to make the strategies easily understandable to our students, we came up with four vocabulary learning strategies: dictionary use, context analysis, word part identification, and mother tongue analogy.

The first step in the study of these strategies was the construction of a reading comprehension questionnaire, which was administered to 35 first-year students on Economics and Management courses at the University of Évora. Fifteen words in the text were selected and grouped according to the use of a specific strategy predicted by the researchers. For each word, the respondents were asked (a) to say if they knew it, providing a short translation or definition if they answered 'yes' and (b) if they answered 'no', to identify the strategy used, as well as to provide a short translation or definition of the word.

The first aspect to be analyzed was the vocabulary known by the respondents. Then, we moved on to the core of the research – the identification of the strategies used when unknown vocabulary was encountered. Our next aim was to verify the level of success of the learners who used the expected strategies and to identify if other frequent strategies eventually led to success.

Conclusions

- There is a gap between what students think they know and what they actually know.
- There is an overuse of the dictionary.
- Even though dictionary use was the most favoured strategy, it did not produce high levels of success.
- Most students did not use other appropriate strategies that might have led to more efficient results.
- Although the dictionary seemed to have been overused, it proved to be a valuable tool when learners did not immediately recognize similarities between certain words and their mother tongue equivalents.

Pedagogical implications

- Students should be made aware of the different strategies available when dealing with new vocabulary and know how to use them.
- Students should be conscious of the pitfalls of relying too much on dictionary use.
- Whenever the use of the dictionary is appropriate, students should be able to use it more effectively, for example by not accepting the first meaning given without checking the context.

E-mail: lspg@uevora.pt (Luis Guerra)
pmendes@uevora.pt

6.5 Creating contemporary fiction for learners

Philip Prowse *Freelance, England*

The history of reading over the last 6,000 years shows how closely intertwined culture and reading are. The value given to reading by different cultures varies and this affects learners' attitudes to extensive reading. Equally the 'culture of learning' within classrooms across the world also varies, creating differing expectations of what reading in a language-learning context means.

We looked at the results of three different surveys of teacher and student attitudes to content and cultural issues.

The first survey was of a group of 42 teachers from ten countries attending an in-service course at NILE in Norwich, UK. While just under half of those surveyed encouraged independent reading outside class, over three-quarters used class readers (the same book for all students). It's possible that this affects the content of readers chosen, in that what are appropriate topics for private reading may not be suitable for class discussion.

The second survey was of 1,887 users of pilot editions of Cambridge English Readers who were asked to indicate their favourite genre. The results were: Adventure 19%, Mystery 16%, Detective 14%, Thriller 11%, Romance 12%, Travel 12%, Science Fiction 8% and Fantasy 8%. What was striking, however, was the variation within responding classes and countries. Students, for example, who liked romance often hated science fiction. Clearly this has implications for the practice of using a single class reader revealed in the first survey.

The third survey was conducted by e-mail with 200 teachers from 30 countries, the majority being on or having taken in-service training courses. The aim was to assess the suitability of contemporary fiction using controversial topics. The respondees were asked to read blurbs summarising ten imaginary readers, and to say whether the topics were suitable for their students. The topics covered were AIDS/HIV, marital infidelity, sex change, gang torture, drug culture, werewolves, civil war, pharmaceutical testing, a James Bond-type thriller and a school massacre. Many respondees made the point that suitability depended on the type of school, and on whether the book was for class or home reading. However, while the survey found seven of the topics suitable, and while there was some regional variation, what was interesting was the wide variation between teachers from the same countries teaching the same kinds of students, between Teacher A who felt that all the topics were suitable, to Teacher B in the same school who found them all unsuitable.

What conclusions can one draw? Certainly that teachers and students are sophisticated consumers of readers who are poorly served by many of the available books, which play safe by appealing to the lowest common denominator – so-called 'burger books'. Equally, it can be argued that original contemporary fiction presents fewer cultural barriers than simplified classics or film re-writes. Students want 'real' books, not schoolbooks, and books with a wide choice of genre.

The session concluded with a handout on writing readers which cannot be summarised here, but which I would be happy to send by e-mail if requested.

E-mail: philip.prowse@ntlworld.com

6.6 Creative learning and teaching with readers

Sue Leather *Freelance, Netherlands*

What's in a story?

The goal of my interactive presentation was to show teachers how extensive reading of original readers can help students to learn English. During the session I talked about original readers written by myself and others; these readers have the primary aim of getting students involved in the story, and only secondarily of 'teaching them language'. This is what I believe makes them effective.

I began by reading part of the first chapter of my level 4 reader *The Amsterdam Connection*. The story is a thriller and the first chapter ends with a dead body. The teachers worked in pairs and answered some questions about the chapter. Instead of reading it, you could play the excellent cassettes that accompany the readers. They are very well read and give the students some variety.

Reading the first chapter is a good way to whet the students' appetite for what comes next. Another way of getting students into a book is 'Choose and Tell.' Teachers chose an original reader that they liked the look of. They then went back to their seats and told their neighbour why they'd chosen it. Was it the cover picture, the blurb on the back...?

The activities above are ways of getting your students into reading, which can sometimes be a challenge. Another way is looking at chapter headings. We looked at the chapter headings of a level 5 reader of mine. Teachers tried it and came up with some excellent alternative titles, but not quite the real one, which is 'Death in the Dojo.'

How does extensive reading help language learning? It was time to talk a little about the research, quoted by Krashen in *The Power of Reading* (1993). Interestingly, the research makes powerful claims for reading not only in terms of vocabulary acquisition, which one might expect, but also in terms of grammar!

During the session, the teachers noticed some qualities that make the readers 'readable' for students:

- good, believable characters
- lots of action
- good opening lines that engage students in the story
- 'hooks' at the ends of chapters that keep them reading
- 'narrative first, language second'.

We moved on to speaking activities. 'Why you should read this book' is about getting students to give short, one-minute presentations on the book they've just read, trying to 'sell' it to their classmates. In this case, again, less is more. Ask students to make it 'short, snappy and memorable'.

I then dramatised part of *Death in the Dojo*, where my protagonist, Kate, is lying on the floor injured. I lay on the floor and groaned while the teachers tried to find out who I was and what had happened. They had two minutes to find out as much as possible about the story by asking me questions. This activity can be used to get students *into* a story, too.

So, what's in a story? ... Incredible potential for creative learning and teaching.

E-mail: exceltraining.sue@planet.nl

6.7 Plenary: Hemisphericity

Grethe Hooper Hansen

One of the frequently voiced worries of our day is that children's power of concentration is being damaged by television. But what appears to be 'attention deficit' may just be a change of thinking style. American psychologist R Shlain claims that there is a massive hemispheric shift underway in more or less the whole population, thanks to television, the computer and the mouse, all of which call for visual-spatial activity in the brain. This is the thesis of his book *The Alphabet versus the Goddess*.

The existence of hemisphericity is still debated in many colleges and universities, whereas in one small pocket of the academic world, dominance of brain, ear, eye, hand and foot can be so easily and swiftly determined that 32 different dominance profiles are now being used by teachers and students to cope with learning difficulties. These can be found in Carla Hannaford's book *The Dominance Factor*. Keynote speaker at the SEAL Conference in 1997 and recipient of various prizes in education, Carla is a physiologist and teacher in Florida, working in Brain Gym or Edu-K, a system of body exercise to balance the brain, developed by Paul Dennison from the Applied Kinesiology of Dr George Goodheart.

Kinesiological testing now reveals that education has been progressively discriminating against an ever-larger segment of the learning population. If Shlain's hypothesis is correct, change in the near future is inevitable. It would seem that over time the growth of technology has narrowed educational focus, and with it, our concept of what intelligence consists in. This is nobody's fault, just the result of a logical error: we have confused the problem (underachievement) with the person. Dr Reuven Feuerstein was the first to smell the rat, when after the Second World War, asked to assign immigrant children of different ethnic backgrounds to schools in Israel, he applied IQ tests and found whole races classifiable as educationally sub-normal!

Educational discrimination is likely to be a major factor behind current social problems such as low achievement, crime, violence, family breakup and chronic dependence on welfare. It can also explain the mysterious rise of the entrepreneur from bottom of the form to head of a world-class industry, the prickly relationship between education and the business world, and the fact that our political solution of more testing only makes the situation worse.

To begin at the beginning, we discovered in the fifties, with the work of Nobel Prizewinner Roger Sperry, that the two hemispheres of the human brain have entirely different skills, subjectivity and ways of working. Reflecting a universe of polarity (male, female; sun, moon; yin and yang), they offer diametrically opposed ways of perceiving the world. There is a dynamic tension between opposites: we understand warm by reference to cold. This polarity is neutral; it becomes duality only when we add the *logical* notion of exclusivity – things are either *a* or *b* – and see it as conflict. In the brain, it enables us to do opposite things simultaneously: when I look at a landscape, I can take in both the whole configuration and its details.

Difference in nature is always balanced by an underlying principle of unity. The two hemispheres of the brain are complementary, dependent on each other and normally unable to work in isolation. The ideal brain state, from a physiological point of view, is one of equal balance, and this is the target of kinesiology. Showing how impossible it is to separate the two hemispheres completely, the chart below was produced by developmental psychologist Sally Goddard, author of *A Teacher's Window into the Child's Mind.* It shows the distribution of functions in a typical classroom task to right or left brain:

		1 Recognition of numbers and symbols	R
2 Find meaning of symbols	L		
3 Register necessary procedure and carry out sequential tasks	L		
4 Hold number facts in working memory	L		
		5 Find a number pattern (e.g. times table) and align numbers in correct columns	R
6 Integrate results in working memory	L		
		7 Recognition of number obtained	R
		8 Test plausibility of answer	R
9 Articulate the answer	L		

The basic difference between the hemispheres is that the left is specialized to deal with detail and the right with a *gestalt*, or whole picture. Accordingly, the left works more slowly, dealing with one thing at a time (serial perception), and the right seeing everything simultaneously (parallel perception). Because a few people have their hemispheres reversed, Carla Hannaford refers to them as logic and gestalt rather than left and right. The logical might be described as the critic, focusing on words and their meanings, identifying, classifying, describing, explaining and reasoning, whereas the gestalt is the receiver of overall implication, dealing with the hidden meaning above and behind words. The major task of the conscious mind is to pick out significant details and distinguish them from the background flux of information and events; this is the foundation of analysis, a separation of one thing from another, the logical way of working. By contrast, the gestalt hemisphere works through synthesis, noting similarities and bringing together things that might initially have appeared quite different, the analogical way of working.

Extremes of Logical/Gestalt characteristics

LOGICAL	GESTALT
Rational approach to the world	Intuitive approach to the world
Logical; sees cause and effect sequences	Analogic; sees correspondences and resemblances
Solves problems by logically and sequentially looking at the parts of things	Solves problems with hunches, looking for patterns and configurations
Makes objective judgements	Makes subjective judgements
Pays attention to differences	Pays attention to similarities
Is planned and structured	Is fluid and spontaneous
Prefers to work with information that is established and certain	Prefers to work with information that is elusive and uncertain
Reads and understands analytically	Reads and understands by synthesizing
Primary reliance on language for thinking and remembering	Primary reliance on images (kinaesthetic, aural, visual) for thinking and remembering
Comfortable with a learning mode of talking and writing	Prefers to learn through experience, e.g. drawing and manipulating objects
Controls feelings	Lets feeling take over
If emotionally sophisticated, can easily label and identify feelings, v. co-counselling	For emotional therapy, prefers bodywork, voice, colour etc.
Doing things: acts in accordance with the structure of the environment	Needs to do things in own way
Comfortable with hierarchical (ranked) authority structures	Prefers participative authority structures
Sequential	Simultaneous
Is a splitter: distinction important	Is a lumper: connectedness important
Talks, talks, and talks	Prefers demonstration and diagrams to words
In learning, the details illuminate the whole	In learning, must have whole picture first
Draws on previously accumulated, organized information	Draws on remembered patterns that are not organized into sequences but cluster around images associated with feelings
Creates controlled, systematic experiments	Creates open-ended, random experiments
Comfortable with multiple choice tests	Prefers open-ended questions for testing

The chart highlights extreme differences between the two modes, but in reality there is a continuum, with one mode blending seamlessly into the other. While we would associate the gestalt with freedom and the logic hemisphere with control, we are all familiar with the paradox, which exists for example in poetry, of providing structure and rules in order to allow a more creative freedom. All successful creativity requires a more or less equal blend of both aspects.

The general rule is that the gestalt tends to be more active in the early stages of understanding and learning, the logical in the later stages, when we focus on certain things and exclude others.

However, each person has an idiosyncratic hemisphericity or preferred dominance, whereby one part of the brain, or one configuration of neurons, responds faster and more intensely to information than another. This changes during the course of a lifetime, but there is some evidence that we do eventually revert towards our initial pattern. In nature, there is a more or less even distribution of hemisphericity, with half the population tending towards the logical and half towards the gestalt, and no hemispheric difference between male and female. The female does have a thicker corpus callosum, the bundle of nerve fibres which separates and connects the two hemispheres; this gives her greater flexibility in alternating between the two.

It is important to understand how hemisphericity is varied and changed by the stimulation we receive. Music offers a useful example: normally, melody, tone and timbre are received in the gestalt hemisphere, rhythm (time segmentation) in the logical. However, a musician is trained to take an analytical approach, learning to separate the elements of melody etc. Gradually his overall response to music begins to show more and more logical hemispheric activity. In a similar way, Shlain showed how literacy, made possible by the creation of an easy-to-use alphabet of only twenty-six letters, changed the thinking patterns of western culture. This resulted (in his view) in progressive discrimination against the female, who is associated with gestalt approaches to life because of her biological role.

Different languages create a different bias. The perception of vowels is associated with the gestalt hemisphere, consonants with the logical (Restak, *The Brain*, 1984). From this arises a speculation that languages which tend to make distinctions through vowels rather than particles and consonants (e.g. Spanish and Italian) tend to encourage gestalt hemisphericity – because, as in the example above, the brain is bathed more often in gestalt hemispheric activity. Those that make distinctions through consonants (e.g. final -*s*) and particles, such as English and German, intensify logical hemisphericity. As an example, take the verb *to eat*:

in Italian:	mangio	mangiamo	In German:	ich esse	wir essen
	mangi	mangiate		du isst	{Sie essen
	mangia	mangiono		er isst	{ihr esst
				sie essen	

While Nature has planned an even distribution, language causes bias across a whole nation, and this is reflected in the culture.

Education and hemisphericity

Carla Hannaford's research shows that what education has assumed to be intelligence is in fact only logical hemisphericity: according to her graph, the children selected as gifted and talented are mainly logic hemispherics, and those at the other end of the scale in remedial education are mainly gestalt hemispherics. Howard Gardner's work on intelligence would indicate that we have selected not only the logical, but a very narrow band within it.

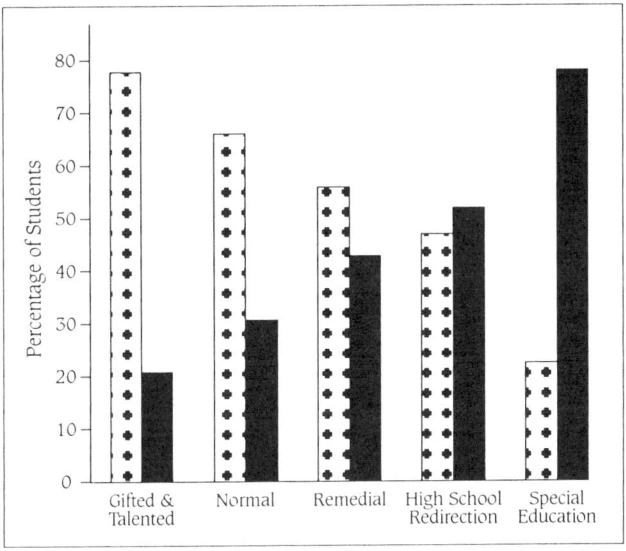

Hemisphere dominance in a random sample of 218 students attending two Hawaii high schools, Denver and Kona. The dotted line shows logic dominants, the black line gestalt dominants. From Carla Hannaford The Dominance Factor.

In the last century the Scottish psychiatrist R D Laing, undoubtedly one of the most brilliant thinkers in his field, was hounded out of Scotland, England and finally even America for his warnings of a similar mistake in mental health. He claimed that many so-called 'insane' patients had as children simply made an intelligent response to a neurotic family environment, and were finally pathologized by a mental health system deeply invested in counter-transference. This was not to say that those patients had not become genuinely ill, only that the system was unable to distinguish between pathology and health-in-compromising-conditions, and its general effect was to make them worse, not better.

To understand the mistake we have made in education, we need to consider the differences in thinking style and learning needs between logic and gestalt dominant. Dr Lozanov, the creator of Suggestopedia[1], has observed that the traditional approach to education is to divide a subject into its elements and teach those elements one by one, as simply and logically as possible, arriving eventually at a composite view of the whole. His approach is the opposite: begin with an overview, deliberately making it difficult, by virtue of very high volume, for the conscious mind to select and separate elements. After presentation, allow incubation time during which the unconscious mind, faster and more efficient, will do the necessary analytical work. This is a reasonable description of the two different ways of working. Lozanov was not aiming exclusively at the gestalt hemispheric; he was simply aware of the fact that a gestalt approach is more useful in the early stages. Montessori had a similar perception, enabling children to develop their cognitive abilities by learning through the manipulation of objects with their hands.

Major needs of the gestalt dominant

Bearing in mind the general *modus operandi* described above, as well as the different characteristics outlined in the first chart, the most important points would be:

1 Speed and freedom from perceptual constraint

Two major characteristics of the gestalt hemisphere are whole-pattern recognition and very high speed functioning, since many different levels of stimuli are processed simultaneously. As noted earlier, the logical hemisphere is much slower, preferring to deal with items serially, one at a time. The gestalt learners' *apparent short attention span* is very often due to the fact that they prefer to work in the high-speed gestalt mode rather than the low-speed, close-focus, analytic logical mode. The restless student *is demanding more stimuli* than a teacher fixed in logical mode is able to give. A slow, logical presentation, which pre-digests information and spoon-feeds it bit by bit, is difficult for the gestalt dominant to take in because there is nothing for the student's brain to do but wait and repeat. Torture for the gestalt student is the teacher covering up the OHP transparency so as to show only one piece of information at a time!

Being so fast in response, gestalt dominants tend to be impulsive, and therefore teachers must expect a certain amount of error, 'carelessness' and mess in their work. Correctness and tidiness are related to slow speed. If you have high speed, you cannot also expect precision and neatness.

2 Whole patterns

The first need of the gestalt dominant is to grasp the whole picture. Without the whole picture, the part is meaningless for a gestalt hemispheric; an analytical presentation is simply bewildering. The gestalt student needs high-volume information, in the form of rich context, charts, diagrams, tables, experiential work, manipulable objects – not the high-focus-and-low-volume, together with its abstractions and reductions, that suits the logical brain. Of course, the gestalt dominant must eventually learn to cope with these things, but the best way to teach them is through a mode of presentation *that allows their brain to function efficiently in its own way.*

When the student fails to understand, the teacher typically *reduces* the information load, a logical response; whereas what the gestalt learner needs in this situation is more, not less, information: more examples, diagrams, illustrations. Reduction deprives the gestalt brain of stimuli and prevents it from working!

3 Idiosyncrasy

A characteristic of gestalt hemispherics is that they need to do things in their own way – in order to arrive at those creative combinations of unlikely elements that are so characteristic. While logic hemispherics are happy to conform to a classroom process, and feel comfortable with uniformity, gestalt dominants, given their high-speed unconscious computations, prefer to choose their own approach. When forced to join in a process they cannot cope with, they are aware in advance that they will fail, but are unable to articulate the problem. They may do as they are told, fail, and accept the denigration that follows – or they may refuse to cooperate.

4 Emotion

Gestalt dominants depend on feeling rather than logic for value-rating (male students may deny this and work hard at disguising their strong feelings as reason!); a high emotional content assists their learning, and a dry factual approach obstructs. By the same token, they are also given to exaggeration, which replaces a more precise use of words to express emphasis or enthusiasm.

5 Need for movement: haptic learner

The learner who has the greatest difficulty with the logical approach to education is the gestalt hemispheric who also has kinaesthetic sensory dominance. 'Haptic' learners respond to the world primarily through body feeling rather than visual or auditory senses. They are even greater misfits in a system that relies mainly on verbal lecture, visual illustration and books. Movement is essential to their learning; you can test this by observing the difference when they are made to stand still or allowed movement when reading aloud.

From the above, it is easy to understand how we have managed for so long to classify these people as stupid. Their different response to stress – which they experience all the time in logical classrooms – only makes the situation worse. Under stress the logical hemispheric focuses down, calms down and concentrates the mind on ever greater detail, appearing more in control. The gestalt hemispheric blanks out, either into frozen stupidity or noisy chaos. Neither response endears them to the logical teacher.

The greatest problem, however, is that their strengths and talents are the opposite of the logicians'. Logic *does not serve their thinking*, given that they most excel in bringing together ideas which are apparently dissimilar; consistency is merely a strait-jacket. Typically, their reasoning process begins with an idea, not a premise; a premise remains constant, whereas the gestalt idea changes constantly. There are no logical steps, just a series of hypotheses, each one very different from ('inconsistent with') the last. Only when they find an acceptable conclusion will they go back and construct an argument.

This frustrates the logician, who sees only tangled wool and an inability to 'reason', accuses them of illogicality and inconsistency, and judges them stupid. Since education supports this judgement, the nearest and dearest of the gestalt hemispherics tend to take the same view; it is not surprising that these students usually have low self-esteem and accept the fact that they are wrong, incompetent and generally unfit for an industrial society.

Boys suffer more than girls because the female, when so judged, can always fall back on the consolation of her femininity. Boys are expected to be rational, logical and unemotional; the taunt of illogicality hurts them much more. To accuse the gestalt hemispheric of illogicality is not only irrelevant and insensitive, but it profoundly negates the quality that is their special gift; this is what makes it so painful. Einstein, perhaps the most famous gestalt hemispheric of all, found a pattern more profound beneath the logic of time and space; no doubt he suffered a number of insults along the way. Our society is full of highly intelligent builders, plumbers, removal men, etc. who were condemned in their first week at school and whose adult minds shy away from the verbal skills demanded in offices. Some escape into the arts, where they flourish, to the dotcoms, and if they can jump the preliminary hurdles, into high finance, which requires the kind of complex mental juggling that gestalt hemispherics excel in. Tragically, many also find their way to the other side of the legal divide.

What can we do about it?

The most useful thing that teachers can do is update themselves on learning styles and intelligence types and share that information with their students, so as to break down prejudice among peers. Once students are aware of their own sensory preferences, hemisphericity and physical dominance, they are better able to appreciate other people's differences. This also makes it easier for the teacher to introduce song, dance and other activities as ways of working with and developing different learning strengths. On this theme, one can make a point of redressing the hurts and insults received elsewhere by singling out gestalt strengths and successes.

To begin every teaching process with an overview changes the life of gestalt dominant learners and does not particularly inhibit the logical students, who can choose to focus down on any one detail. Rich context can be confusing for the extreme logician, who may find it a 'muddle' and be unable to separate wood from trees, but a sensitive teacher can manage to present an overview and a breakdown side by side.

Changes of modality are essential for the gestalt dominant: pictures and diagrams, gesture and movement, dramatization and emotional content, music to stimulate the right brain, song, poetry, drawing – all the things that Lozanov does so well. Unadulterated verbalization sends them into bewilderment or sleep. Make sure you also provide brain gym breaks. (Exercises can be found in the Dennisons' *Edu-K* or Carla Hannaford's *Smart Moves*.)

Of course, gestalt dominants need the skills of logic and organization to survive in our present culture – and there is nothing that most of them want more. A gestalt hemispheric who has developed logical skills has a formidable intelligence, and to enter this world is a transformational experience – as is the logician's progress into visualization. The important thing is that a person must always be taught through their strengths and not their weaknesses: one might begin, for example, with the *story* of the hare and the tortoise, show the advantages that hares can gain from tortoises, and keep the teaching in this *context*, illustrating logic with plentiful *diagrams*.

Until the concept of hemispheric limitation is fully understood, other issues such as self-esteem cannot be dealt with in any meaningful way: no amount of Circle Time can help the extreme gestalt hemispherics with kinaesthetic sensory dominance, because their teachers, peers and even family members already believe that these poor creatures are not too bright, and any work that is done will be subtly contaminated by this belief. Can we as teachers open our minds sufficiently to sweep out the cobwebs of those preconceptions based on a lifetime of mis-belief?

This is just one of the many challenges that face us as education begins the painful transition from an old-paradigm to a new-paradigm world, now lumbering into motion almost one century after the quantum revolution.

Workshop

In the workshop that followed the plenary, participants first answered questions on a handout to identify their hemisphericity, and then lined up so that we could see the dominance distribution of the group. Needless to say, the heaviest weighting was at the gestalt end of the scale (the workshop was advertised as 'highly experiential'); the person with the most extreme gestalt dominance was a lady from Peru – at the end of the scale. The university teachers tended towards the logical, but some of them had had to change dominance to be there. One Russian teacher, who had clearly moved from right to left, was elegantly dressed in different patterns of black and white – which spoke volumes to me! One man, an extreme logical hemispheric who was nevertheless left-handed, seemed to be one of the rare people with reversed hemispheres. It is of course no accident that such a workshop attracts people with hemispheric issues.

A triad was then formed with people of different dominance to discuss another handout on different styles of argument and reading. We did some singing-and-movement to observe our reactions to modality change, and some brain gym, once again to notice our responses. A discussion then followed on how to teach the gestalt dominant, and this displaced the last activity, which would have been a circle dance. Circle dance requires uniformity, which is uncomfortable for the gestalt learner, and it is always interesting to observe the different reactions: try it yourself!

Note

[1] Now called 'Desuggestopaedia' – see Editor's note on p 76

References

Dennison P E & G E (1987) *Edu-K for Kids*. Ventura, CA: Edu Kinesthetics
Restak R M (1984) *The Brain*. New York: Bantam Books

Some useful books

Asher J (1988) *Brainswitching: A skill for the 21st century.* Los Gatos, CA: Sky Oaks
Damasio A (1994) *Descartes' error.* London: Picador
Davis R D et al (1994) *The gift of dyslexia*. New York: Perigee
Hannaford C (1995) *Smart moves.* Arlington, VA: Great Ocean
Hannaford C (1997) *The dominance factor.* Arlington, VA: Great Ocean
Lakoff G & M Johnson (1980) *Metaphors we live by.* Chicago: University of Chicago Press
Shlain L (1999) *The alphabet versus the goddess.* New York: Arkana Books
Pelletier K R (1978; 1985) *Toward a science of consciousness.* Berkeley, CA: Celestial Arts
Vitale B M (1982) *Unicorns are real.* Carson, CA: Jalmar Books

7 TEACHER TRAINING AND TEACHER DEVELOPMENT

7.1 The changing face of English: Implications for training

Sebastian Watkins and Frances Hughes
The British Council, Sultanate of Oman

This talk outlined some of the difficulties encountered by teacher educators on teacher training programmes such as the Cambridge CELTA course, with candidates from backgrounds where English is spoken as a 'second' language. Even at interview stage the dilemma for a teacher educator can be fairly acute: does the applicant speak and write fluently in English, even though their variety of English has its own distinctive identity? Is this distinctiveness so marked that it affects intelligibility in the classroom or the appropriacy of the models provided for language input? This distinctiveness may be evident in diverse forms: grammatical, phonological, lexical or discoursal.

Once candidates are accepted on a CELTA course, these dilemmas persist. Educators may question their right to correct or comment on distinctive features of candidates' classroom language, whether it is incidental language or language being focused on in the lesson. For example, a teacher may repeatedly use the 'catch all' question tag *isn't it?* with a distinctive, sharply rising intonation, or use the word *thrice* to mean three times. (These are both possible features of Indian English.) An educator is thus placed in a quandary with socio-political implications, which is further exaggerated if s/he happens to be an English RP speaker.

Guidelines set by the validating body, in this case UCLES, specify a level of English which 'enables candidates to follow the course' and an ability to use language in the classroom which is 'clear and coherent and free of mistakes'. These are valid criteria, but do not necessarily fully address the issues of the changing face of English.

Political correctness might suggest that educators accept all varieties of English, however distinctive, thus bypassing some of the awkward dilemmas outlined above. However, this talk argued that it might be in the candidates' (and their future students') interests if programmes such as the CELTA were to raise trainees' awareness of their own language features, something they are rarely conscious of. This would enable new teachers to make informed choices about the language they use in various situations, allowing them to code-switch when necessary between their own variety and one more appropriate in a given context, be it the classroom, or in a formal situation such as a job interview. As such, this process might be viewed as a form of political empowerment for some, highly necessary in societies less tolerant of distinctive varieties.

Consciousness-raising should extend to *all* candidates on teacher education programmes, alerting them to the fact that they merely speak a variety of English, whether it is a British regional dialect, Australian or Indian English, or a more 'standard', prestigious variety such as RP. The following could help to raise the profile of own-language awareness:

- comparing pronunciations, i.e. candidates compare their own version with a taped version
- comparing written English, with a particular focus on lexical and discoursal choices in formal written genres
- input sessions focusing on the issue and encouraging debate
- providing an explicit rationale for tutor focus on candidate language during teaching practice

E-mail: sebastian.watkins@om.britishcouncil.org

7.2 Task-based learning and teacher training

Karl Kaliski *International House, Spain*

Background

Despite the reservations of many concerning a presentation–practice model, it is still the dominant paradigm on many pre-service teacher training courses. However, while task-based learning (TBL) has been around for some time, its influence on pre-service training courses (such as CELTA) has been limited. When TBL does appear, it is usually confined to the end of the course and discussed as an optional extra which trainees might like to try at a later date.

The aim of this presentation was to report on a pre-service training course, designed and implemented over the last year, which gives much greater prominence to TBL. This is achieved in three related ways:

- lesson modelling
- teaching practice
- new input sessions

Lesson modelling

In order to make sense of TBL, trainees need a basic template for a task-based lesson. On the second day of the course, trainees explore a lesson model which shows them how to build a lesson around a task. First they experience a task-based lesson as 'learners' and then a questionnaire discusses the principles which underpin this type of lesson. We have found that trainees can make sense of these principles – provided that they are discussed at a level appropriate to a pre-service course. Generally speaking, trainees also relate well to the strong emphasis on communicative language use that this kind of class promotes.

Teaching practice

Armed with a template for a task-based lesson, trainees also require plentiful opportunities in teaching practice to experiment with TBL. At the start of the course, they are given teaching practice points which enable them to do so. Depending on the length of classes to be taught on any given day, trainees may teach all or part of a task-based class (which may then be continued by the next trainee). Later on in the course, trainees have more opportunity to design task-based classes of their own.

New input sessions

We also felt that a number of new input sessions would help trainees work more successfully with TBL. A key issue in TBL concerns how to incorporate a focus on form. A number of input sessions explore this area, showing trainees how to work reactively with the language learners produce and how to exploit texts for post-task language focus work. Further input sessions also offer trainees a range of task types they can use to design task-based classes and explore how to apply TBL to coursebooks.

Findings so far

The response so far, from both trainee teachers and teaching practice students has been very positive. It is clear that trainees can plan and manage lessons built around tasks, although creating – and taking – opportunities for a focus on form remains a challenge. Trainees also enjoy the opportunities that TBL offers to communicate with students as real people. On the strength of the courses run so far, we would argue that TBL deserves a much more prominent place on pre-service training courses than it has had to date.

E-mail: kkaliski@teleline.es

7.3 The Lingua A Project ILIAD: A new multi-lingual approach to self-directed INSET

Anton Prochazka *Centre for Information on Foreign Language Teaching and In-service Training, Austria*

Overview

The International Languages Inset At a Distance (ILIAD) Project, with partners in the UK (Open University, CILT), Sweden (University of Karlstad), Spain (Instituto Cervantes), France (IUFM des Pays de la Loire, IUFM de Paris) and Austria (Pädagogisches Institut des Bundes in Wien, Centre for Information on Foreign Language Teaching and In-service Training), is creating a web-based, interactive network of communication and a resource bank for pre-service and in-service language teacher training across Europe, in conjunction with the BBC. The development is a Lingua A Project funded by Socrates.

Aims

- to raise awareness of what is culturally specific in language classrooms in different countries
- to compare and link primary and secondary school practice in the teaching and learning of foreign languages using practical examples
- to complement existing training materials (pre-service and in-service) used in partner countries

- to increase positive attitudes amongst learners and teachers towards ideas from other places and countries
- to raise awareness of how language teaching methodology is affected by cultural factors
- to stimulate discussion with others

The four issues

The following four issues, which focus on two sub-themes each, are common in all five partner countries:

1 Motivation (Motivating Factors, Teaching and Learning Approaches)
2 Planning (Planning Teaching Sequences and Classroom Management)
3 Pupils Learning Languages (Pupil Autonomy, Does grammar matter?)
4 Resources (Resources 1 and 2)

Expected benefits

ILIAD is now in its third and final year. It brings together pre-service and in-service providers, teacher trainers, teachers and their learners in developing both a communication network of language teachers and a CD-ROM to address the above-mentioned issues. In Year 1 the BBC filmed 15 different classrooms in five European countries. Basically it is a bank of texts, video and audio, based on classroom teaching of four different languages (English, French, German and Spanish). There are two ways in which the resources are organized. You can look at those resources developed in each country (country path) or you can explore them by looking at the language taught (language path). During the second and third years of the project, a network of integrated teacher groups in each partner country worked on the same task from different perspectives in order to analyze classrooms and to put all their findings on the CD-ROM.

Outcomes

The ILIAD resource will include multimedia and multi-lingual training resources targeting key aspects of the language curricula at late primary and early secondary levels from each partner country. The technology will enable users to move from one resource to another, one language to another, and one topic to another, thus making links between approaches and philosophies of different teachers in different countries. It can be used for pre-service and in-service training, by groups of teachers or by individuals. More information on ILIAD can be found on the following website: www.cilt.org.uk/iliad

A number of dissemination activities are already being planned, among which will be the one-and-a-half-day International ILIAD-Symposium, to be held from 29 to 30 November 2001 in Vienna at our institute. This will not only be a unique opportunity to get to know the newly developed CD-ROM and to exchange experiences with colleagues and experts from various parts of Europe, but will also offer experiences in real classroom teaching in different Viennese schools. Why not come and join us at the presentation of this innovative self-directed INSET CD-ROM in Vienna?

E-mail: anton.prochazka@pib-wien.ac.at

7.4 Training the trained: Accommodating experienced teachers on CELTA courses

Fiona Hardy *Solihull College, England*

Increasing numbers of trained and experienced teachers are applying to follow a CELTA course in order to take their career in a new direction. As CELTA is designed as a pre-service training course, its syllabus is not suited to the needs of candidates seeking a change of direction within teaching. Trainers assume, fairly, that CELTA trainees come to the course needing to acquire a whole range of skills and competences, ranging from the procedural, such as classroom management, to the theoretical and pedagogical. However, many of these can be assumed in the case of teachers seeking to continue in the profession while changing subject area. Obviously, the extent to which a teacher comes prepared to teach EFL depends on their subject specialism; a teacher of modern foreign languages can be expected to have skills that are germane to the teaching of EFL, whereas the gap is greater to bridge for those coming from other subject areas.

As a trainer, I have noticed that the blend of trained and novice teachers is not always a happy one and can cause the latter group to feel they are at a disadvantage, the trained having a head start over them, in particular in terms of classroom management. My experience of such situations has led me to observe that novice teachers' prevailing problem at the start of a course is their lack of confidence in teaching practice, something that experienced teachers tend not to suffer from to anything like the same extent. From the perspective of the trained teacher, much of what is covered at the beginning of the course is already familiar to them, areas such as lesson planning, formulating aims, reflecting on their classroom practice, amongst others. This can make them feel impatient with the course, creating further difficulty in terms of group dynamics.

It is an oversimplification simply to note the negative aspects for the untrained of being combined with candidates who are already trained. The experienced teachers can offer much assistance to their untrained colleagues. Furthermore, the trained may have some 'unlearning of bad habits' to undertake, something which demands a high degree of awareness of their current practice and a mind open to new, different ways of teaching and learning.

Bearing in mind the above points, it may be that an adaptation of the CELTA course specifically to meet the training needs of experienced teachers could offer a quicker route to trained status for those with classroom experience and do away with the issue of combining them with novice teachers. Such a course would reduce the focus on the procedural aspects of teaching and put more emphasis on the theory of language learning and its practical application in the EFL classroom. It would be delivered differently, with these 'experienced' trainees being given a mentor (an experienced EFL teacher trainer) to work with over a 25-hour-long course that would consist essentially of teaching practice, feedback, observation of experienced EFL teachers and tutorials.

E-mail: fiona.hardy@solihull.ac.uk

7.5 The wood or the trees? Classroom observation and effective teaching

Deniz Kurtoglu Eken *Bilkent University, Turkey*

Classroom observation is an essential training tool for promoting effective teaching. In order to ensure its effectiveness, however, it needs to be based on a principled approach to supervision and a shared set of appropriate teaching criteria.

Among the many principles for effective supervision in pre- and post-observation meetings are the following: building the teacher's confidence and providing support; exploring the teacher's beliefs about teaching and learning and perceptions of self and students; promoting the idea that the observation is focused on the *whole* lesson; finding out about the class and the students; encouraging the teacher to reflect on her/his lesson and being genuinely interested in what s/he has to say; highlighting strong points and being honest about these; and discussing alternative teaching strategies for areas highlighted for further development (not just saying, for example, 'Try to focus more on your error correction techniques').

In addition to the above principles, it is crucial in both oral and written feedback, for the trainer to adopt a positive attitude right from the start (considering the time and effort the teacher has put into the lesson and the idea that there is always something 'good' in every lesson); to refer to descriptive information to support any comments made; to use sensitive language, focusing on the present or the future, *not* the past (e.g. 'You could nominate different students.' instead of 'You could have nominated different students.'); to maintain a balance between ideas suggested and ideas elicited (i.e. not always 'giving' or not always 'eliciting'); to identify a maximum of two or three main areas for the teacher to focus on and to ensure that these are 'grounded' in the comments made; and to use a dialogue style in written comments (i.e. *not* addressing the teacher in the third person).

In order to ensure effective supervision, the above principles need to be supported with criteria which allow for holistic exploration of the lesson and not just an analytic focus; an effective observer needs to see both 'the wood' and 'the trees'. Such an approach necessitates the use of holistic tools rather than checklists. Instead of assessing each and every individual quality or skill, the observer can usefully focus on some main categories, provide specific feedback under each, but assess the lesson and the teaching as a whole. The extract below exemplifies the criteria that the presenter has developed on the basis of research with teachers, students, and trainers at Bilkent University School of English Language and that are currently being used in the school. Due to limitations of space, however, only one example is provided under each category.

Knowledge and awareness

- knowledge about students (e.g. names, abilities, interests, affective and cognitive needs, class dynamics)

Planning and preparation

- choice of techniques/teaching strategies (e.g. appropriate to students' needs and interests, motivating)

Rapport and communication with learners

- ability to motivate students to learn (e.g. expressing genuine interest in students, reacting/responding to students, valuing students' contributions, using humour)

Lesson execution

- elicitation/questioning techniques (e.g. varied, challenging, motivating)

Lesson management

- monitoring and providing support where necessary (e.g. encouraging students to think, guiding but not doing the work for the students)

E-mail: kurtoglu@bilkent.edu.tr

7.6 Classroom observation for trainee teachers

Lia Luminita Blaj *Western University of Timisoara, Romania*

Classroom observation is widely acknowledged as indispensable in preparing trainee teachers for their future professional activity. How classroom observation should be carried out, however, is far from being a matter of general consensus. An approach to this practical component of trainee teacher education is proposed by Wajnryb (1992), who sees classroom observation as a skill that can be acquired and used as an efficient tool in learning to teach.

At the Western University of Timisoara, due to the very limited time allotted to the TEFL course, students have so far not been formally introduced to observation skills and strategies. As a beginner teacher trainer/educator, working in the context of an extended teacher training/education schedule, I attempted to design an introductory module to equip future EFL teachers with classroom observation skills before they undertake their pre-service teaching practice.

The ten-hour observation skills module, piloted with 15 trainees, was designed to achieve the following objectives:

1 *learning about teaching* – in the sense of acquiring action-system knowledge, see Leinhardt, Putnam, Stein and Baxter (1991)
2 *raised awareness through reflection on experiential knowledge* – which relates to a professional's ongoing experience according to Wallace (1999)
3 *reflection rather than imitation* – favoured by Wallace (1999), who sees teaching as professional action
4 *active involvement* – of the trainees in the practicum
5 *trainee autonomy* – an inquiry-based rather than prescriptive approach to the practicum
6 *metalanguage* – in line with Good and Brophy (1997), who claim that 'Conceptual labels are powerful tools in helping teachers to become aware of what they do.'
7 *good professional relationship* – between the trainee and the school-based educator
8 *springboard for further professional development*

The observation skills and strategies (after Day 1990, Nunan 1989, Riley 1996, Wajnryb 1992, Wragg 1994) to which the 15 trainees were introduced and which they practised during the ten-hour module were:

- choosing focus of the observation activity
- becoming aware of expectations before the observation
- deciding on method of data collection: freehand notes logged in order of occurrence, narrative account, tape-recording, observation schemes, diaries
- recording data objectively
- categorising and classifying data
- reflecting on data
- formulating questions starting from the data and looking beneath the surface
- drawing conclusions/formulating insights gained
- applying observation instruments/schemes critically
- setting up own observation tasks
- drawing up a coherent plan of observation
- building data bank

The audience were invited to question and comment on the appropriacy of the skills selected. They were then given excerpts from diary entries written by the 15 trainees after applying the observation skills to the school-based component of their teaching practice. Comments from the audience, though supportive of the idea of observation skills for pre-service teacher training/education, underlined the time constraints. My conclusion after piloting the module, supported by trainee feedback, is that it will work best if offered as an option and intertwined with the university course and seminars, and not delivered on its own.

E-mail: liablaj@mail.dnttm.ro

7.7 Giving feedback on giving feedback: Towards a more structured approach

Rachael Roberts *Solihull College, England*

In this talk I attempted to define what skills a trainer in training needs to develop, particularly when giving oral feedback on teacher training. I also presented some sample tasks to help develop some of these skills. I considered the stressful and potentially threatening nature of feedback, and how this can trigger negative and hostile reactions in a group of trainees, and looked at strategies to minimize these effects.

I suggested that confusion and lack of structure can provoke anxiety, and therefore that, just as a lesson will have a basic outline, a feedback session can also benefit from this kind of design. To focus on this, the trainer-in-training could be asked to set the agenda for observation by considering their own aims and timing. I also looked at Wajnryb's (in *SIG Selections* 1997) framework for feedback, and how this could be used to develop observation tasks. I referred to the work of Bion (*Experiences in Groups* 1961) and Schutz (*A three-dimensional theory of interpersonal behaviour* 1958), exploring how group dynamics theory could be applied to working with groups of teachers-in-training. Schutz suggests that there is a predictable series of interpersonal issues to be resolved in any group: inclusion, control and affection. The issue of meeting inclusion needs could be addressed by tasks looking at patterns and extent of interaction, and the actual language the trainer uses. Diane Phillips' research into positive politeness strategies (in *SIG Selections* 1997) relates closely to inclusion. Once people are satisfied they belong, control issues start to surface. For the trainer this means the ability to encourage reflection and a learner-centred approach, balanced with being sufficiently informative and supportive. Too much support can create what Bion calls a dependency group, in which the trainer is held responsible for everything – including failure. Too little, especially for a novice teacher, can be overwhelming, leading to negative responses. I looked at Gebherd's Models of Supervision (in *TESOL Quarterly* 1984), and considered how these could be used as a basis for observation tasks to reflect on the trainer's style, particularly what they do compared with what they think they do. Schutz's third set, affection needs, relate to considering the trainees' need for acceptance. One way trainers may deal with this is again through the language they use. (For example, Diane Phillips' research into negative politeness strategies, which attempt to disassociate the hearer somewhat from the 'wrong' behaviour.)

Body language can also be a useful clue to how much a trainee can 'take'. We can develop more sensitivity to this by observing the non-verbal signals of closing up: turning away, folding arms and so on. A useful task here is for the observer to monitor the behaviour of a 'difficult' trainee. Focusing on the situation from the other person's point of view can help the trainer to put aside their own feelings of being threatened and thus be better able to help the struggling trainee. In such ways as these I suggested, we can start to move towards a more structured approach to training trainers.

E-mail: rachael.roberts@solihull.ac.uk

7.8 Giving feedback at a distance

Anne Kennedy *Freelance, England*

The workshop began by considering how the following affect the delivery and acceptance of feedback:

- channel
- setting
- participants
- content
- time frame
- objectives
- perceptions and expectations

We discussed the role that feedback has played in our personal and professional lives; compared giving and receiving feedback on distance and face-to-face programmes; considered both formative and summative feedback, trainee expectations of courses, the language we use to praise, make suggestions and diminish isolation; and the frames within which course participants operate.

We looked at guidance slips as a method of giving feedback, and at tutor comments. We considered which to use, which to modify and which to discard. The comments we analyzed ranged from the brief *...you might like to consider...* to the lengthier *...we can adopt an alternative approach which I attach here for your consideration...* From this task arose the question as to whether wordy politeness strategies might be considered too complex and confusing for participants whose first language is not English. Although this question remained unresolved, our discussion took us beyond considering the words we use, to perceiving that what we write cannot be separated from the cultural, social and educational contexts within which the recipients of feedback operate.

When reading a selection of comments from course participants on a distance learning programme, it was noticed that anonymous comments had a tendency to be less positive than identifiable ones. Do trainees fear that honesty will prejudice their results?

Some input was given pertaining to the concept of 'frames' referred to in Russell & Munby (*Teachers and Teaching* 1992). This led to consideration of why feedback is not always accepted in the spirit in which it is given. Is negative feedback linked to an inability to operate within any frame other than one's own?

We felt that the following outcomes from the workshop merit consideration. When giving feedback at a distance:

use inclusive language:

- 'we' not 'you' when considering response improvement
- 'you' when giving credit for success
- use phrases which show understanding
- highlight common ground
- give encouragement

make feedback objective:

- use check boxes to give feedback on tasks
- attach guidance slips to suggest alternative/improved responses

ensure there is:

- transparency of evaluation criteria
- clarity of own objectives
- acknowledgement of the participant's contribution
- validation of what is correct
- correction of inaccuracies
- discovery of merit in incorrect responses
- room for discussion
- avoidance of nitpicking over minor details
- allowance for individuality
- focus on informational content of tutor feedback

In obtaining course feedback consider:

- inclusion of tasks in worksheets which promote feedback
- changing tasks which produce confused/inaccurate responses

- providing genuine opportunities to express feelings about a task/module/unit
- eliciting feedback on tutor comments/guidance slips/reports

In conclusion, we decided that in considering alternatives for our own feedback methods on distance learning programmes, course administrative costs, logistics, tutor time and tutor pay (per hour or per course) could not be ignored.

Some feedback – at a distance – on the suggestions and the session would be welcome.

E-mail: a.kennedy@eurolinkcourses.co.uk

7.9 Teacher development in language lesson planning

Maria José Flores Carpe *Secondary School 'Felipe de Borbon', Spain*

This workshop developed as follows:

The first point was to define the concept of Teacher Development according to our previous ideas and to incorporate new ones pointed out by some of the participants. This led to the central concept: TD is a process of changing our preconceptions or previous ideas about our way of teaching and learning, so as to improve our professional practice.

After that, thoughts about the 'good language teacher' were not difficult to define. Just to mention a few of them:

Teachers as:

- developers of new techniques
- facilitators, good listeners, guides in a learner-centred environment
- motivators, giving the students the opportunity to make decisions and experience things for themselves in an encouraging learning atmosphere

Once these general considerations were established, the audience was ready to begin with the 'Language Lesson Planning', in which they were asked to list aspects of their work that were well done and things they felt they could develop better in future. Some examples were:

Skills I can manage very well:

- designing tasks
- creating a non-threatening environment
- listening to learners' needs
- reflecting on my practice

Skills to improve:

- planning lessons thoroughly in advance
- training students to be more autonomous
- organizing more cooperative groups
- developing new materials

One of the things that the audience had no doubt about was the crucial role played by motivation and self-esteem in the classroom.

> *Motivation is the most important factor for success in language learning. It is even more important than specific ability in languages.* (Gardner 1985)

Regarding language lesson planning itself, different activities were identified, within a common frame:

- warm-up activities
- new work (based on previous work)
- oral exercises (with concise explanations)
- practical applications (communicative interchange)
- preparation for home study (for the next class)
- end with a relaxing task

Each of the above was developed and put into practice as in the classroom. At the same time, a brief reflection on textbooks was discussed according to their appropriateness for teacher and student, language and language context, grammatical coverage, etc.

Once the textbook had been considered and the language lesson planning had been revised, another point was to design activities according to our students' different preferred learning styles. These were outlined, including the following:

visual	studial	dependent
auditory	experiential	independent
kinaesthetic	analytic	global

The use of authentic materials was also an important aspect to consider when planning a lesson in which students' own identities, needs and hopes are involved.

Finally, in considering teacher reflection, we agreed that reviewing our practice on a daily basis and making necessary changes are important tools for teachers. Keeping a diary is also a good way of providing a record of teaching ideas and problems experienced, which can lead to long-term professional development.

To summarize, the audience was given a questionnaire to reflect upon the way we teach (self-evaluation) and to help them think about our own process of teaching. This questionnaire highlighted for some teachers the strategies needed to improve our practice in an effort to teach according to our students' expectations.

E-mail: MARYJOAL@inicia.es

7.10 Introducing classroom research to in-service teachers of English in Russia

Radislav Millrood *University of Tambov, Russia*

This report is based on experience in Russia's teacher development projects sponsored by the British Council in Moscow.

Exploratory teaching integrating research and pedagogy is an effective way towards turning a teacher into a reflective practitioner. Yet teaching is seldom accompanied by research efforts leading to better classroom insights. Typical obstacles are the 'Why?' (*Why should I do the research when I see no benefit in it?*), the 'How?' (*How should research be done while avoiding unnecessary investment of time and effort?*) and the 'What?' (*What to choose as an object of research?*)

These obstacles were to be turned into opportunities by developing in teachers critical thinking, introducing to them techniques of classroom research and enhancing their professional expertise through structured reflection.

Critical thinking was interpreted by the teachers as an intentional, careful consideration of any belief, opinion, knowledge, stereotype, principle or script in the light of concrete evidence, supporting or refuting it. An indication of critical thinking was teachers' ability to address their classroom situation with narrowly focused questions.

Teachers' problems could arise from lack of approach, lack of materials or lack of insight. Lack of approach prompted the teachers to engage in theoretical reasoning. Lack of materials required materials writing and piloting. Lack of insight called for the generation and interpretation of classroom data.

Classroom enquiry comprised both qualitative (non-numerical) and quantitative (numerical) research. Interestingly, teachers preferred quantitative research to qualitative data collection. One of the reasons was that quantitative data was easier and quicker to obtain in order to produce a general picture. The alternative way was to focus teachers' attention not only on the general, but also on the particular, and to give them training in conducting qualitative research.

An important research method was teachers' action research, i.e. an active attempt to improve one's classroom situation and to reflect upon the findings in a structured and systematic way. The teachers were introduced to the following steps of action research: goal setting, hypothesis formulation (if–then, either or, not–but), literature review, selecting and administering treatment, data elicitation and analysis, impact evaluation, conclusion and recommendations.

As a result of training, the teachers focused more attention on problems arising from using techniques and activities in the classroom, as well as on producing their own materials. The ratio between theory, teaching material and classroom insight became more balanced (originally teachers' projects were dominated by descriptions of material). At first, classroom problems of the 'short-circuit' type were prevalent, i.e. 'problem–remedy–experience'. After training, classroom problems of the 'acme type' emerged, such as 'problem–experience–insight'.

Teachers' research training experience was summarized in the poem produced on reflection at a training session:

Nobody forced me to undertake this journey.
All the way I found it challenging and trying,
Until I reached the top of the mountain
And looked down.
And saw farther…
Broader…
Deeper…

E-mail: millrood@millrood.tstu.ru
Homepage: http://tsu.tmb.ru/millrood1/index.html

7.11 Viewing the whole manager

Jonathan Gore *The British Council, Syria*

Teachers as managers

One of the key management issues that was raised at the conference was the implication of the fact that teachers who performed well were often promoted to management positions with minimal or little training. Further to this, there were a number of talks and workshops which raised the subject of what the qualities of a good manager are, and how those qualities can be revealed. Two examples were presentations by Shelan Rodger and Jane Dancaster.

Upward appraisal and resistance

My own talk examined the area of upward appraisal and how managers are viewed by those they manage. This is a contentious area, which tends to raise a considerable amount of management resistance. Chief objections to staff expressing views on the manager's qualities are that 'subordinates ... lack the information needed, are inexperienced, inflate ratings to avoid retaliation, rate harshly and undermine the manager' (Williams 1998).

What can staff assess?

It was conceded that not all qualities can be judged by staff; however, there was agreement at the talk that certain qualities (competences) could be so assessed. We discussed examples that I introduced of some of the British Council competences: interpersonal skills; communication; flexibility; delegating effectively; leadership and teamwork; client and customer relations. It was agreed that there were a considerable number of competences which staff were able to assess.

How can upward appraisal take place?

Various methods were discussed, including appointing a facilitator to interview staff and obtain views, through internal reports, questionnaires and training courses. The issue of anonymity also arose. Some felt that anonymity was essential, others that this could lead to untruths or irresponsible statements. It was agreed that whatever took place should be set against a background of trust, and required training and counselling.

I introduced a questionnaire I use in Syria, where I manage two centres, one in Damascus and one in Aleppo. This is distributed to all staff. It is a simple list, against which staff grade '0' (never) to '5' (always). The form is reproduced here:

The Teaching Centre Manager:
- listens to me
- gets back to me on matters raised
- follows matters up
- evaluates my work
- allows me to make suggestions
- gives weight to the suggestions I make
- acts promptly

- is supportive
- delegates and explains fully
- produces clear written procedures
- provides clear structures to operate in his absence
- provides clear systems regarding designation of responsibility
- deals with me fairly
- criticizes where necessary
- effectively manages the line management system
- makes clear my financial and resource duties
- takes an active role in my career planning
- provides sufficient opportunities for training.

My contention is that all managers need this kind of feedback in order to manage effectively, and that upward appraisal should become a standard benchmark of a well-run educational organization.

E-mail: jon.gore@bc-damascus.bcouncil.org

7.12 Plenary: Teaching English is a political act: A non-P.C. dialogue

Gabriela S Matei and Péter Medgyes

Motto:
'A language has nothing to do with politics.
Or it shouldn't.'
A teacher of English

1 Introduction

'In our age, there is no such thing as keeping out of politics,' said George Orwell in 1946. This statement rings true in our day more than ever, and we are convinced that education in general, and TESOL in particular, is charged with political implications. Hence the title of our presentation.

In order to find out whether our belief is shared by others in the profession, we opened it up for international discussion by inviting colleagues to respond to a multi-item questionnaire. We sent out the questionnaire to teachers we knew, but we also posted it on electronic lists, such as ELTeCS-L. So far we have received feedback from 103 teachers in 29 countries. It is only fair to mention that this is an exploration in progress, which we wish to continue, even though we are aware that the project will not yield definitive answers.

'Political' and 'politics' are terms with multiple and often ambiguous meanings. For example, 'political' is used to describe particular ideas and allegiances, such as belonging to a political party. 'Politics' is used today in contexts like 'he resigned because the firm was full of politics', implying power struggle, manoeuvring for position, etc. What is important is that we perceive these terms as very much connected to *power* and *status*. For the purposes of our presentation, however, we adopted Kirk and Broussine's (2000: 14) definitions:

Politics = a set of beliefs, principles and commitments which drive our actions and interventions.
= a means of acquiring and using power to create the societies and organisations we want.

'Political' is also used in the phrase 'political correctness', or P.C. for short. Our presentation carries the sub-title 'a non-P.C. dialogue', because we do not automatically accept current or past orthodoxies in TESOL. Instead of striving to be P.C., we will simply present the views of our respondents and our own on three issues: *Global English*, *Teacher Power* and the *Status of English Teachers*.

In addition, our questionnaire included questions concerning ELT coursebooks and English teachers' associations and conferences, but as we did not have the time to elaborate on these areas during our plenary, we have decided not to include them in this paper.

2 Global English

In the midst of an unprecedented boom in English language instruction, the question arises: Should TESOL teachers rejoice in their good fortune or develop a guilty conscience? Or, as we formulated it in the questionnaire:

> English has become the global language of our age. As professional teachers of English, should we rejoice or apologise for the role we play in spreading English, often at the expense of other foreign languages? What do you think?

In an issue of *The Budapest Post*, an English-language weekly, Hughes (1992) meditated over the paradox of English teaching in Hungary. She asked, 'Are we accomplices in the blanketing over of an erstwhile *super culture* by a *superculture*?' Her answer was a resonant *yes*. Rejecting this attitude as liberal crap, Cheng (1992) argued that English, like any other lingua franca from earlier times, enriched rather than obliterated local tongues and local cultures. Therefore, his suggestion to fellow American teachers in Hungary was as follows: 'We should count our blessings instead of flagellating ourselves.'

As it turned out, our respondents were similarly divided over this 'tricky' issue. On the one hand, there were the 'rejoicers'. In case anyone should query that TESOL is imbued with politics, here is a quote with an express political allusion: 'In a word, once used by Margaret Thatcher, rejoice.' In justification, some respondents referred to the common good: 'We're performing a useful service to help people function in the world today.' This being the case, 'we should take pride in being able to play this role,' someone added. There were several respondents who adopted a client-centred attitude, as it were, by emphasising that 'If students come to a class to improve their English competence, then that's what the teacher should focus on.' Still others shamelessly admitted that the mere fact that there was plenty of work available for TESOL teachers was a good enough reason to celebrate.

In sharp contrast, there were colleagues who apologised for the ubiquity of English in the contemporary world. 'It's sad that the "weed" that is English might snuff out other languages in the "Language Garden",' somebody argued, but the ante was upped by this radical comment: 'I see the rise of Chinese with huge relief. Maybe we'll be saved from the further extension and penetration of Imperium Americanum by the oldest continuous culture on Earth.'

Some of our respondents adopted a middle-of-the-road approach. One of them noted, for example, that we should 'rejoice as long as what we're spreading is a pluralistic view of Englishes, [and] apologise for the linguistic imperialism.' Another person mentioned that though she had her personal remorse, she need not apologise for something (i.e. the spread of English) which was beyond her control – a point reiterated by several others. Indeed, we might ask, would it be fair to hold the erstwhile Russian teacher responsible for the fact that Russian had been made the compulsory and often the only language permitted in the school curriculum of several countries which once belonged to the sphere of the Soviet empire? This would be just as unfair as to blame the hamburger boy at the McDonald's round the corner for the universal spread of McDonaldisation, wouldn't it?

The majority of respondents, however, do not regard this as an either/or issue. In addition to stressing the pragmatic role that English plays, they believe that it is a tool for promoting better understanding among different cultures, for dispelling linguistic misunderstandings between nations, for enriching one's own culture and language, and so on. 'I hope the future is one that celebrates the polyglot' – a wish we warmly welcome in the European Year of Languages and afterwards.

In summing up this section, it looks as though attitudes to the issue, and to several others, may be represented on a triangle, with *the pragmatist*, *the professional* and *the moralist* situated at the vertices:

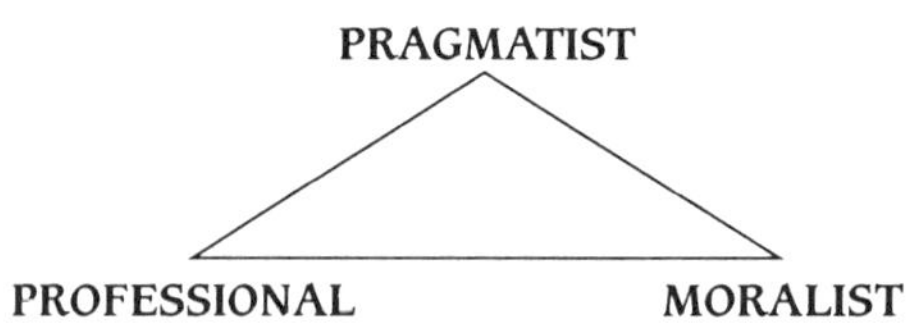

All teachers are located somewhere within this triangle, including our respondents – as this section attempted to demonstrate. The authors like to think that they are closer to the professional than to the pragmatist or the moralist. It would be interesting to find out where the readers of this paper picture themselves.

3 Teacher power

Our respondents were invited to answer the following questions:

> In your opinion, is there such a thing as 'teacher power'? How would you define it?

When we were devising the questionnaire, we assumed that 'teacher power' would be a provocative term – and we were right. Our survey showed that the concept really existed, even though it generated definitions which were often in conflict with one another.

3.1 Reactions to the term 'teacher power'

Although most respondents tried to define 'teacher power', some voiced ambivalent feelings towards the term, or even towards the concept itself. Some argued, for instance, that the term was too strong or sounded like a 'buzz word' while others perceived it as downright negative; 'I cannot really relate to this coinage,' one respondent said.

3.2 Teacher power: real or imaginary?

With only four exceptions, all respondents answered 'yes' to our question regarding the existence of teacher power. There were nuances of positive responses though, ranging from the enthusiastic 'Indeed, there is!' through the firm 'Yes, definitely' to the neutral 'Yes'.

Those who gave a negative response either expressed their regret that teacher power was no longer what it used to be, or by implication that society no longer accorded 'respect for the education process'. 'If this power existed,' one of them wrote in a more humanistic vein, 'then the best exercise of that power could only be in not exercising it.'

3.3 Definitions and taxonomies of teacher power

We synthesised the definitions offered by our respondents in the table below, together with a few illustrative quotes for each category:

Teacher power defined as		Quotes from the respondents
1	influence	'Teacher power might be defined as the teacher's influence (for good or ill) on his/her learners.'
2	control	'Teacher power = teacher's control over what's going on in the classroom.'
3	knowledge	'Our power is our knowledge and the ability to transfer it.'
4	personal qualities	'Charisma', 'ability to communicate', 'wittiness', 'sense of humour', 'enthusiasm', 'love'.
5	ability to empower the students	'It is a power to empower students to learn on their own.' 'The power to challenge learners to question received ideas.'
6	teacher solidarity	'Lobbying', 'Joining peers to struggle for improved working conditions.'

Although the respondents in our study did not make clear distinctions between the concepts of 'power' and 'authority' as they appear, for example, in Cohen and Manion (1989: 203), it is remarkable that many of them were conscious of the dangers of wielding power. For instance, a respondent warned that power is 'a dangerous temptation for the language teacher'; someone else pointed out that 'power easily breeds dictatorship', and yet another warned of the consequences of misusing teacher power: 'Teachers can often be thought of by students as terrors!' In fact, several colleagues reiterated that teacher power can become negative, especially when teachers 'impose thoughts and information on their students', or when 'teachers manipulate students'.

3.4 Degrees of teacher power

One item in the questionnaire inquired about the degree of power the respondents claimed to possess in the various contexts and communities where they worked and lived. As we expected, the place where our respondents perceived themselves as having the most power was in their own classrooms, although as one teacher put it, 'It depends on which of my classrooms I'm in.' It is worth mentioning that the place where they felt least powerful was the university: 50 per cent of the respondents who worked in universities claimed to have 'no power' in their own institutions.

3.5 Final thoughts on teacher power

'Teacher power' is such a loaded term that some teachers did not even feel comfortable using it. Despite such reservations, however, the underlying concept was perceived as very real by the vast majority of the respondents (96 per cent). While some teachers seem to have had no qualms at all about being powerful in their professional environments, others denied the legitimacy of teacher power, unless it referred to empowering students. A third group of teachers deplored the fact that they did not have enough power, or regretted the loss of teacher power: 'I don't think I wield power any more. At our place the regulations have almost completely rid the teachers of any personal power.'

On the other hand, it was generally agreed that the power teachers had in the society was negligible. One teacher wrote: 'If you consider teacher power in society, teachers are far from being powerful,' while someone else emphasised that this social disempowerment might lead to the humiliation of teachers: 'Once the teacher has left the classroom or the lecture hall, in most cases s/he becomes anonymous, if not even humble or humiliated.' We believe that all these have profound implications for teacher status (see Section 4 below).

In our dual role as authors of this study and as practising teachers, we argue that teachers need a lot of power for their work and indeed enjoy a good deal of power – in their classrooms at any rate. The point is that, at least in the cultures where the authors of the present study come from, students expect teachers to be powerful figures, not only in terms of professional qualifications, abilities and knowledge, but also in terms of personality: students wish to be impressed and entertained, and they appreciate teachers with strong, if not charismatic, personalities. At the same time, we concede that this power must be exercised in compliance with high ethical and professional standards, mainly to the benefit of the learners, but also to that of the teacher him- or herself. Basically, we agree with the respondent who wrote: 'If the teacher is powerful, then the students are powerful as well.'

4 The status of English teachers

In this regard several questions (and answers) spring to mind. How much are we TESOL teachers worth? How do we compare to other professionals? Why is TESOL held in low esteem in most parts of the world? Who are the lucky exceptions? Provoked by such puzzling questions, we included two items in the questionnaire to broaden our horizons. Let us deal with them separately.

4.1 Compared to other teachers

Seeking information about the relative status of English teachers in the staffroom, we asked this question:

> In your opinion, are there any differences between a TESOL teacher's social status as compared to the status of (a) other subjects, and (b) other languages? If yes, what do you think generates such differences?

As the percentage of 'no' responses was less than ten per cent, we thought it would make more sense to restrict the scope of investigation to the 'yes' responses.

First of all, it was generally accepted that English is the unparalleled lingua franca of our times, 'the language of Bill Gates,' as someone put it. 'English is seen as a passport to a "better" life,' said another colleague; (the use of inverted commas for "better" may have been an oblique hint that the gatekeeping role of English was not universally welcome). To be sure, English was seen as a vital commodity exposed to fluctuating market forces, with the implication that the face value of TESOL increases if there is a shortage of English teachers and decreases if there is a surplus. 'In our country,' said one respondent, 'English teachers enjoy a higher status for their scarcity value'; in certain places teachers were even regarded as a status symbol.

While most colleagues agreed that 'better marketability is the only feature that separates us from other teachers,' others offered a list of professional traits, both positive and negative, to spell out these differences.

Indeed, what advantages do TESOL teachers have over their fellow members of staff? Many respondents stressed, not surprisingly, that English was a popular subject and students were motivated to learn it. In several places, TESOL teachers had better opportunities to travel, develop their professional expertise and earn better salaries (even if this involved having to take on second and third jobs). At the same time, there were repeated references to certain virtues characteristic of the TESOL teacher. For example, they were perceived to be streetwise, flexible and easy-going, to have a flair for networking in general and establishing interpersonal relationships with their learners in particular, to be open to innovative ideas and sustain high standards of craftsmanship. Furthermore, 'we are attached to the "citizens of the world" kind of stereotype' – whatever this epithet means.

On the debit side, TESOL teachers were often labelled as 'the necessary evil in the staff who fluctuate, are part-timers, and not faithful to the classical educational teacherly roles.' This reminds me (Peter) of a story a young English teacher from Budapest told me recently. Not long after she had started working in a secondary school, she was accosted by an elderly history teacher: 'Tell me, love,' she asked, 'will you be staying long enough for me to try to remember your name?' This turned out to be a prophetic question: soon afterwards the young teacher left the school for a secretarial job where she was offered a salary three times as high as her school salary. Be that as it may, Alan Maley's comment that TESOL is a permeable job should apply to quite a few countries in the world.

Returning to our questionnaire, a colleague had this to say: 'English in the school curriculum is perceived as a waste of time and state school teachers as having a poor command of English.' On the lighter side, somebody remarked that 'English teachers are of course not as clever as teachers of maths' (thank you), while another respondent, rather curiously, claimed that 'maths and physics are masculine subjects, whereas English is a feminine subject.'

Native speaker teachers formed a distinctive group by espousing a gloomy view. Working abroad as a native speaker teacher, one of them claimed that 'there lingers an idea that any backpacker who is fit for nothing else can become an English teacher,' a belief borne out by the intermittent surge of unqualified youngsters teaching English as a temporary source of income. Hence the cynical comment: 'In some countries saying that you're a native speaker teacher is synonymous with a tourist who didn't want to leave.'

While some expatriate native speaker teachers felt frustrated, their peers working in the UK described a bleak picture. 'Employers perceive us as temporary labour rather than as professionals,' someone noted, and this opinion was expressed even more grimly: 'We're seen rather as outsiders, non-conformists, weird.' If any non-native teacher ever toyed with the idea of emigration, this is hardly a turn-on, is it?

4.2 'Pay us enough to buy a good car!'

Although TESOL teachers were often found to have better opportunities than teachers of other subjects, they were certainly not assigned pride of place. To ascertain the validity of this assumption, we asked a second question concerning the status of teachers:

> As an ELT manager we know said: 'If you want to raise teachers' status, pay them enough money so they can buy good cars.' What do you think about this?

This was meant to be a provocative question and, judged by emotional responses given in the questionnaire, it succeeded in arousing a great deal of interest. Instead of embarking on a thorough analysis of the responses, let us just offer below a sample of quotes arranged in two columns: one for the positive and one for the negative reactions.

Agree

- Absolutely agree.
- Certainly, that should be part of the package.
- Yes, why not? Money is not evil.
- Tell me where and I'm on my way.
- I can't drive. I don't own a car and have never wished to ... I still feel I'm criminally underpaid.
- Money is not always the solution – though it helps.
- I don't think I understand. It should be: 'so they can buy enough food.'
- If people died because they didn't know English, teachers would be paid better.
- A lot of truth in it, alas! I'm ashamed to be seen correcting homework on the bus.
- Teaching is an option for a desperate situation if the trainees can't find anything else.
- If there was a strike at last, I'd be the first to join.

Disagree

- Stupid.
- Nonsense.
- Must have been an American.
- Presumably this manager was a 'primitive new Russian' type, or maybe they were just joking.
- In Germany the car is a status symbol, yes, I'm a cyclist.
- I couldn't feel comfortable in a society where the size of cars determines social status.
- Teaching is a calling, a new monasticism, but the outside world doesn't understand this.
- Cynical! But the message about the need for societies to demonstrate that they value teachers is important.
- A car without a professional is not enough to raise teachers' status.
- Whoever loves teaching will stay in the profession irrespective of quantity of pay.
- A good salary is not going to make bad teachers better.

To summarise our views on the issue of the status of teachers, we believe that better salaries would make our profession more competitive and more attractive for young people to choose it as a long-term career. After all, it is very doubtful whether without adequate financial means teachers can command the respect of contemporary society and maintain a level of self-esteem required to pursue this profession. At this point, we can't help recalling Dry's wry message: 'A sure recipe for low learner performance is to set up a situation where the learner pities the teacher, and then pities himself for being saddled with a pitiable teacher.' (Dry, 1977: 200).

5 Conclusion

This paper has aimed to demonstrate that TESOL is a political act, and very often flies in the face of the dictates of P.C. views and expectations. Our assumptions were based both on our own experience and on the experience of an international group of teachers.

So who are we TESOL teachers? Are we a boon or a curse? Are we the imperialists or the liberators? Do we merely provide a service, or broaden the mind and tend to the soul? Do we have more or less power and status in the school and the society than we deserve? It seems that there are more questions than clear-cut answers.

To be sure, we play three main roles in the classroom and beyond: those of the professional, the pragmatist and the moralist. All of us are trying to strike a balance between these three roles, although by no means do we give them equal weight. What we consider more important than the proportions of the three components is that every teacher acts independently and to the best of their beliefs, thus preserving their personal and professional integrity.

We would like to end this journey into the cultures of teaching English by expressing our desire to replace the image of the powerless, passive teacher with an image of the powerful, active teacher, who is ready to assume the role of a decision-maker and a 'transformative intellectual' (Giroux, 1988), a 'connoisseur' rather than a 'proletarian', an 'image of prestige' rather than an 'image of disrepute' (Foster, 1997).

Let us conclude with our favourite quote:

'A group of 18-year-olds once presented me with a little crown-like object made (by them) of metal and beads. It distinctly reminded me of a crown of thorns. The inscription said: "The teacher affects eternity. She can never tell where her influence stops." I still treasure this present and I still can't think of a better definition.'

Acknowledgements

We wish to thank all the teachers who took the time and effort to fill in our lengthy and provocative questionnaire.

References

Cheng D (1992) Are teachers accomplices in imperialism? In *The Budapest Post*, December 3–9.

Cohen L & L Manion (1989) *A guide to teaching practice* (3rd ed.). London: Routledge

Dry D P L (1977) Whose motivation and to what end? In *ELT Journal 31/3*: 195–202

Foster K (1997) *Proletarianization and connoisseurship of teachers*. Available at http://www.coe.uga.edu/quig/proceedings/QUIG97_Proceedings/Foster.html. [accessed on 21 October 2000]

Giroux H A (1988) Critical theory and the politics of culture and voice: Rethinking the discourse of educational research. In R R Sherman & R B Webb (Eds.), *Qualitative Research in Education: Focus and Methods* (pp. 190–210). London: The Falmer Press

Hughes F (1992) Cultural imperialism? Nonsense. In *The Budapest Post*, 20 October–4 November

Kirk P & M Broussine (2000) The politics of facilitation. *Journal of Workplace Learning: Employee Counselling Today, 12(1)*, 13–22

Orwell G (1946) *Politics and the English Language*. Available at http://eserver.org/theory/politics-and-english-lang.text [accessed 10 October 2000]

8 INFORMATION AND COMMUNICATIONS TECHNOLOGY

8.1 Integrating training in basic Web skills with English language instruction

John Pill *The British Council, Hong Kong, China*

The Internet is changing the ways in which we access information. In the 'information age', skills are more useful than knowledge; effective search strategies are more useful than memorized facts. People need the skills to find the information they want, as members of society and as enquiring individuals. Exploiting the World Wide Web fully probably means using it in English. Currently, however, there is little information specifically for learners of English about using the Web effectively. Nevertheless, many Web skills have a linguistic element, making them appropriate for EFL/ESL classrooms.

Warschauer and Healey (1998) describe these skills as 'electronic literacy skills' (*Language Teaching* 31: 57–71). I propose that tasks to develop them should be linked with course content. Teachers can integrate them into lessons as another syllabus 'thread', just as they include learning strategy work or study skills.

WWW addresses and jargon

a) Students match site addresses with their topics (e.g. www.un.org with United Nations), becoming sensitized to the use of suffixes to indicate location, and acronyms or abbreviations. Students then predict addresses for sites themselves, checking them, using a browser.

b) Students create posters or 'guidebooks' to explain the Web jargon, acronyms, and country/domain-name codes they meet.

Search engines – listings, keyword searches, search results

a) Students look at categorized listings (e.g. under 'Directory' at www.google.com) and consider the decisions needed to select a path through them to find specific information. They then decide which of the sources offered is the most 'trustworthy' or current.

b) Students research a given topic on the Web by choosing suitable search terms for a keyword search. Initially they choose from a given selection; later they decide on terms to search with themselves.

c) Refining searches with synonyms can involve register, e.g. 'heart attack' and 'cardiac arrest'. Do the two sets of results indicate anything about usage here?

d) Using truncation and wildcards highlights British/American spelling differences and demonstrates the importance of prefixes, suffixes and word roots in English.

e) Evaluating a list of 'hits' involves recognizing the language of each site; determining the relevance of content using textual clues (e.g. synonyms, expected phrases and names); and checking from its address if the site is a personal homepage or something more authoritative.

Navigation – layout, hyperlinks; evaluation

a) Students consider what a well-designed website/webpage looks like and produce a checklist to evaluate sites.
b) Hyperlinks are a type of linguistic reference. Students decide where hyperlinks lead (within/outside the page/site) and then check. Can users assume that links outside a site are as authoritative as the original site?
c) Students add links to a text, showing they recognize main topics and when additional information would be useful.
d) Students develop criteria for site evaluation, perhaps considering issues of authority, bias, coverage, presentation/layout and language level.

Teachers can work to develop a comprehensive list of Web skills for language learners. They need to keep up-to-date to support learners, since the Web is constantly evolving. Computers are important learning tools; their integration into classrooms demands new skills from teachers and students.

E-mail: johnpill@iohk.com

8.2 Perceptions of the integration of CD-ROMs into classroom lessons

Justin Kernot *The British Council, Italy*

With the increasing amount of language learning software being used in language classrooms, CALL has become a popular area for research. I conducted a study to investigate the perceptions of students and teachers of the use of CALL as an integral part of lessons in a language classroom and its effectiveness as a learning tool at the British Council, Hong Kong.

A fundamental issue was computer training, a lack of which resulted in students and teachers shying away from using computers. Formalized training would encourage more standardized computer awareness among learners and teachers. Troubleshooting skills would build confidence in teachers who are afraid of losing control in the classroom should a technical problem disrupt the lesson. Awareness of new software and how to use it would lead to more fluent use of programs by teachers and students. A systematized training programme to deal with these areas of computer training might help to encourage more integration of CALL software, but would also enable teachers and students to become better evaluators of CD-ROMs and, therefore, to be able to identify the effectiveness of certain programs over others.

With computers built into the desks, the physical set-up in the 'Classroom of the Future' at the British Council in Hong Kong allowed CALL software to be a part of the lesson which linked to the other stages as seamlessly as possible. In the future, it is foreseeable that many classrooms will adapt and take on a similar design. Such integration allows the physical barriers to be lowered and facilitates the inclusion of CD-ROMs as a part of a 'whole' lesson.

Trends in EFL teaching have moved in recent years towards a more student-centred approach, with learner autonomy being encouraged. Results and implications indicated that software programs give learners increased control in terms of pace and material. The learner can navigate his or her own way around a program, check answers, explore grammar rules, test himself/herself, look words up in a glossary and read the tapescript of listening texts. Such facilities are more and more becoming a part of programs produced and encourage more learner autonomy as more facilities are made available. It would appear, then, that the integration of CD-ROMs helps to train learners to study and explore language more independently and should be encouraged.

It is evident that as multimedia software is now readily available in many institutions, thought needs to be put into how to harness this technology and encourage its use as an integral part of lessons. Students and teachers perceive CALL software as a useful and positive part of learning and teaching, but their doubts and fears appear to have held back the effectiveness and regularity of integration.

E-mail: Justin.Kernot@britishcouncil.org.ae

8.3 Writing with a dictionary in book form and on CD-ROM

Birgit Winkler *Open University, England*

This talk referred to a study that examined how an English learner's dictionary, in book form and on CD-ROM, is used for writing. It investigated students' dictionary skills and revealed how effective such dictionaries are.

Thirty upper-intermediate/advanced students at British university English-language centres participated. After completing an introductory dictionary tour and questionnaire, students wrote briefly on a general topic, accessing firstly book and then CD-ROM dictionaries. I recorded all look-ups and audio-taped students' think-aloud protocols.

About two-thirds of participants consulted the CD-ROM dictionary more often, finding it easier, quicker and more convenient. However, look-ups per (monolingual) dictionary were maximally 12, minimally 0 (four students claiming never to use one for writing). Meaning was a key criterion in using both dictionaries; spelling came second, then grammar, collocation and lexis (varying frequency for the two dictionaries).

Most spelling and half the meaning problems were solved with either book or CD-ROM. Two areas were problematic: lexis – viz. synonyms, collocations and words unknown in English – and the CD-ROM's advanced search facility.

Both dictionaries helped students with spelling only if initial word-letters were known; the elicitation CD-ROM lacked a Spellchecker, but its special Wordwheel – in which users are taken steadily closer to their search term as more letters are entered in an onscreen box – was advantageous.

Long entries, phrasal verbs and idioms caused some difficulty in meaning, as did look-ups demanding cross-references, and where information was lacking (new words). Many students could not interpret and ignored codes, symbols and abbreviations, inferring grammatical information they needed from examples. Prepositions, reflexive verbs and word-formation rules also caused problems. Generally, students had difficulty handling typographical conventions (/, ~) and technical terms, such as 'register', 'idioms' and 'phrasal verbs'.

Otherwise, students missed their bilingual dictionary since 'how can you look up a word you do not know in English'?

The CD-ROM's advanced search facility putatively supports users in finding items related to their search term, scouring the entire dictionary text for every word-token. Refined searches use filters or Boolean operators. Yet depending on the search term, the search results list was either too long (overwhelming), did not provide what was required, or offered nothing at all: such searches exploit lexical forms, not (semantic) meaning. Only familiar and experienced users can carry out such complex searches. Most searches for collocations and synonyms were unsuccessful. Thus, students either left the original, rephrased a sentence or chose a familiar word.

Students' dictionary skills and the dictionaries themselves could both improve. To become effective, users need training; CD-ROM dictionaries, particularly, require additional navigational and searching skills. A change of attitude towards dictionaries may also help, as students were apparently unaware of the monolingual dictionary's value for writing.

The vast storage of a CD-ROM could beneficially encompass further materials, e.g. technical terms, synonyms, cultural details. Search facilities should allow information access and retrieval in ways that would complement the dictionary's internal, traditionally alphabetic organization, e.g. by theme. Finally, future hybrid forms of bilingualized dictionary would help English learners find unknown words – which they cannot look up monolingually.

E-mail: B.Winkler@open.ac.uk

8.4 Extending the use of standard office software in ELT

Marc Loewenthal *College of North West London, England*

This presentation aimed to show how, with some thought and imagination, word processing and presentation software can be used more extensively in CALL teaching. While there is a huge amount of authoring and dedicated software available, the costs and licences may be too expensive for many individuals or institutions to afford. If they already have office software, it can provide them with a platform for developing useful and varied activities with a degree of interactivity and at no additional cost.

Most word processing software is now so powerful that there is far more to it than just word processing, spell checking, punctuation practice and so on. Matching and gap-fill exercises and activities can be made by using text boxes, which have the advantage of being independent of the page and can be manipulated through dragging and dropping. They can also be coloured and sized. Clip art can also be placed in text boxes and manoeuvred in the same way, and call-outs (speech bubbles) have the same properties as text boxes. Sound can also be added to text, for example, to demonstrate pronunciation, and pages can be linked together with hypertext links placed in the page, so that students can refer to answer pages while studying alone. With some time, exploration and imagination, teachers can produce numerous activities tailored directly to their students' needs.

Presentation software is generally used as a medium for individuals to make presentations to audiences, though it can also be used for automatic and continuous presentations on computer. It is not generally exploited by teachers, but it can provide useful practice in speed-reading, especially in preparation for exams in which fast and accurate reading is essential. To do this, the teacher would have to learn to use the software to make a presentation of a few slides. This presentation is to be shown on the computer screen as the reading text. A separate sheet with the tasks and questions (tick the box, write in a word, etc.) should be word processed and given to the students on paper for preparation in class.

The slides in the presentation should have automatically set times before transition, so that students only have a fixed time to read each one, for example, three minutes. Students can be conditioned to reading within a set amount of time because they know the information will soon disappear. In a long-term reading programme, a large number of presentations can be made, with one or two practised every few days, and the length of reading time shortened by a few seconds each time. Individual paragraphs can also be introduced at fixed intervals within each slide. Graphics and images can be added. All this helps the students to get used to reading quickly and effectively.

If anyone would like samples of material demonstrating these ideas, and more detailed instructions, please e-mail the address below, and I will be glad to provide them.

E-mail: rainer@marcloe.freeserve.co.uk

8.5 Using writing software with children and teenagers

Emma Arthur *Stavanger University College, Norway*

This presentation illustrated how supportive writing technology can be used to develop and support the writing skills of young learners of English aged 7–14. The main emphasis was to show how specific programs can be tailored to meet the needs of different learners, and in particular children with learning difficulties.

Supportive writing technology includes word processors, wordbank software, word predictors, motivational programs, talking word processors and programs with speech output facilities. Speech recognition was not discussed. The aim of this type of software is to enable learners to become more independent by compensating for some of the limitations and difficulties they have during the writing process. This enables children to produce a higher quality and quantity of written work than is possible using pencil and paper.

After looking at considerations in using software, three programs were presented in detail – *Clicker 4*, *Penfriend for ELT* and *Storybook Weaver*.

Clicker 4

This program is an easy-to-use multimedia authoring program, which allows teachers to create professional, tailor-made activities to support any course book. Speech, sound and video can be used to create materials to develop reading and listening as well as writing. Activities such as matching, talking books, story writing, sentence work, ordering, grammar, vocabulary work, true and false and spelling can be designed. *Clicker 4* was initially designed for pupils with special educational needs in UK schools, but work with the program has shown that it can successfully be used with EFL and EAL pupils. It is the flexibility of the program which has made it so popular.

Penfriend for ELT

This program addresses the needs of pupils with dyslexia and writing difficulties. It is a prediction program containing specially designed lexicons which children can use while they are writing. Teachers can tailor the lexicon to suit the writing task. *Penfriend for ELT* can be used together with any word processing program and appears as a small window on the screen. During the writing process, relevant words appear in the window. Children can click to hear the words before inserting the one they want into their writing. The program also reads back what is written if required. *Penfriend for ELT* helps dyslexic pupils in a variety of ways, but perhaps most importantly, children gain confidence and feel they can produce a piece of writing to be proud of.

Storybook Weaver

This piece of software is an easy-to-use multimedia tool, which allows pupils and teachers to quickly create professional-looking stories. Its database of images and text linked to speech capability allows children to tape their own voices and create their own talking books. This is a very motivating program and will encourage even the most uninterested pupil to write. Used along with *Penfriend for ELT*, it has the potential to enable pupils with writing difficulties to achieve a good piece of writing.

If you would like more information about the programs above or other programs for young learners of English, I can be contacted at the address below.

E-mail: emma-a@online.no

8.6 Learning the hard way: Strategy use and on-line distance education

Nicky Hockly *The Australian Institute, Spain*

Distance learning (DL), especially e-mail based or on-line distance learning, is all the rage. However, very few courses publicize how difficult doing a distance course can be, and DL is often subject to a heroic 'legitimizing' discourse.

Research (e.g. White 1995) has shown that in comparison to traditional classroom learners, traditional (print-based) distance learners (DLs) tend to use more metacognitive strategies, and also more affective strategies, given that opportunities for using social strategies are far fewer. White also suggests that distance learners use more affective strategies to *compensate* for the lack of social strategy use available in DL environments. My own research has confirmed that traditional DLs use very few social strategies, and that affective strategy use remains problematic for both weaker and stronger learners.

I would like to suggest that using an on-line learning environment (OLLE) as a support to a print-based DL MA in TEFL programme gives learners the chance to develop both affective and social strategies, and makes for an enhanced DL experience. Making participation in the on-line part of a DL course compulsory immediately excludes those learners with no technological access; thus, in my context, use of the OLLE remains optional.

The role of the OLLE, as it cannot form part of the assessment of learners, thus has a dual function: to help create a 'community of learners' in which social and affective strategy use may come into play, and also to promote a constructivist approach to the knowledge content of the course (where learners can work in small groups on collaborative tasks, both social and academic). I am currently working on trying to achieve this through the following means:

- a month's orientation to the OLLE *before* learners receive any course content
- using this month to focus primarily on the forging of personal links among the learners themselves, and with the course tutors ('climate-setting') e.g. through an on-line pre-course questionnaire in which learners are given space to voice affective issues such as fears and doubts about the course, etc.
- a 'Who's Who?' section in the OLLE for which learners are given tasks
- icebreaker activities which focus on getting learners to work initially on simple tasks in pairs, then in small groups (here the focus is primarily on the process of group formation)
- addressing context-specific anxiety issues, such as the use of English (an L2 for over 90% of our learners, who are based in Spain and Latin America). The learners debate a protocol for language use (English, or Spanish, or both?) in the OLLE
- trying to mitigate the stress caused by on-line work (e.g. through lack of technological know-how; decreasing motivation during the course; not being able to 'measure' one's achievement against colleagues') by specifically addressing these issues in tasks and discussions.

E-mail: nicky@funiber.org

8.7 Supporting and evaluating distance learning students' use of an electronic discussion board

Alice M Oxholm *Sheffield Hallam University, England*

The TESOL Centre Diploma currently has a 40-week paper- or CD-ROM-based distance learning phase, followed by a four-week full-time direct contact phase at Sheffield Hallam University. The students are, typically, experienced native speaker teachers of English, working individually overseas.

Electronic conferencing provides a new context for learning and interacting, where both tutors and students are creating and shaping the learning environment (Salmon G, *E-moderating* Kogan Page 2000) and it was envisaged that the *Discus* discussion board would enable and encourage students to post-up questions/comments on modules and talk about tasks with other members of the group. A questionnaire was used to identify the students' computer background and canvass them on the tools. This showed all the students to have access to a computer, either at home or at work. While previous experience of ICT, e-mail and the Web was high, the majority of the group had little experience with other forms of electronic communication.

Tasks were allocated to the students each week, and these can be divided into three types: Social, Academic and Technical (Salmon 2000). It was anticipated that the main role of the tutor would be to set the tasks and moderate the responses.

Over the six-week trial period, student participation dwindled and there were very few new participants. The majority responded to tasks set in the early weeks where they were asked to comment individually on their work and give an example of their teaching. Responses and comments to each other were minimal, the main contribution being isolated responses to tutor-set tasks. It was found that a good amount of tutor time was spent responding to individual student questions and encouraging interaction.

A second phase of this research has been set up to examine these questions in more detail. A café area is now available for online socialization, to allow students to become familiar with the environment prior to being asked to exchange academic information. The academic tasks are now integral to a specific distance learning module, chosen for the level of student-perceived difficulty.

The success of moderation appears to be dependent upon a number of factors. In the light of this, tutor intervention and its effect on student response needs to be examined further. Students need access to adequate resources and technical competence, and the software tools should be robust. The type of task set has a bearing on the perceived relevance and level of difficulty for the student and this can affect the degree of participation and satisfaction.

Tutors need to develop a clear sense of their audience and the composite needs of the group. There are implications arising from this for the training of online tutors. In particular, student reticence in contributing, despite expressing enthusiasm for the tools, must be overcome for effective and integral use to be made within a course. Our research will continue to investigate this area and participants were invited to take a look at the discussion board at: http://www.shu.ac.uk/schools/ed/public_html/discus/index.html

E-mail: a.m.oxholm@shu.ac.uk

9 CLOSING PLENARY

Twenty-first century English

David Crystal

English language teachers always have to be prophets – that's prophet in the sense of prophesying not profit-making, of course. Typically, young students are being introduced to a language by somewhat less-young teachers, whose responsibility it is to provide their charges with a set of linguistic abilities that will meet their future needs. If I found myself teaching a class of fifteen-year-olds, in some nightmare, I would not want to be teaching them how to speak 59-year-old Crystallese. I would want to be giving them a take on the language which was more compatible with their own age, and the age of young adulthood which they were about to enter, and that would mean my taking into account the usage trends around them. Teachers obviously have to teach the language as it has been and as it is now; but they also need to keep a wary eye on the linguistic future – the kind of language their students will find themselves experiencing some years from now. It is not easy. Teachers are always having to make judgements about the chaos of language variation and change which they find around them – which usages are trivial, which ephemeral, which significant, which long-lasting. It is a difficult task because predicting the linguistic future is full of uncertainty – and it needs special help. Doubtless some people rely on supernatural assistance to do it (and thus make my analogy with prophets particularly apt). You have done something just as sensible: you have joined IATEFL.

The fact of the matter is that, at any moment, the language might change and a particular rule or recommendation become out of date. Wise teachers therefore always pay special attention to those aspects of English which signal possible, impending, or ongoing change in the standard language – the differences in dialect usage which can be heard or seen within a country or between countries; the distinctive usage which accompanies the arrival of new activities within society; the areas of disagreement, or disputed usages, which surface among native speakers; or the letters of complaint which are sent to the press or the BBC. Of course, not all kinds of variation will result in changes in standard English: some developments in society are always going to be more influential than others. And even linguists can be taken by surprise at the unpredictability of a change. But sometimes a particular trend stands out above all others, and then it is well worth taking time to reflect on it. My topic today is one such. I believe it to be the trend which is going to have the greatest impact on the English language during the twenty-first century: computer-mediated communication, and specifically the Internet.

The Internet, as we all know, is an association of computer networks with common standards which enable messages to be sent from any central computer (or *host*) on one network to any host on any other. It is now the world's largest computer network, with over 100 million hosts connected by the year 2000, providing an increasing range of services and enabling unprecedented numbers of people to be in touch with each other through electronic mail (*e-mail*), discussion groups, and the provision of digital 'pages' on any topic. There is no denying the unprecedented scale and significance of the Net, as a global medium. The extra significance is even reflected in the spelling, in languages which use capital letters: this is the first such technology to be conventionally identified with an initial capital. We do not give typographical enhancement to such developments as 'Printing', 'Publishing', 'Broadcasting', 'Radio', or 'Television', but we do write 'Internet' and 'Net'.

What is it like, to be a regular citizen of the Internet, a *netizen*? Those who already spend appreciable amounts of time online need only self-reflect; for those who do not, here is a short selection from various Web pages headed 'addicted to the Internet':

- You wake up at 3 a.m. to go to the bathroom and stop to check your e-mail on the way back to bed.
- You sign off and your screen says you were on for 3 days and 45 minutes.
- You placed the refrigerator beside your computer.
- You say 'scroll up' when someone asks what it was you said.
- All of your friends have an @ in their names.
- You tell the cab driver you live at http://123.elm.street/house/bluetrim.html
- Your phone bill comes to your doorstep in a box.
- You check your mail. It says 'no new messages'. So you check it again.

With so many people spending so much time on the Internet, especially in an interactive way, the effect on language is bound to be immense – and immediate. In the old days, it might take decades for a new usage to find its way around the globe. Today, new usages can be everywhere within minutes. All languages with an electronic presence are therefore going to find themselves changing faster than ever before – and English, as the still dominant voice of the Internet (recent surveys suggest it accounts for some 70% of Internet traffic, though the figure is rapidly falling as other languages come on-line) will change more than most. The nature of the electronic medium as such, along with the sheer global scale and intensity of Internet use, will result in developments that will be far more pervasive and momentous than in the case of previous communication technologies. The arrival of print, the telegraph, radio and television each gave language fresh dimensions that generated many new distinctive varieties and usages, from the telegrammatic graphic prominence of newspaper headlines to the hyperverbal sonic prominence of sports commentaries. The electronic medium will have a much greater impact because it presents us with a channel which facilitates and constrains our ability to communicate in ways that are fundamentally different from those found in other semiotic situations. Teachers are used to thinking of English in terms of 'spoken English' and 'written English' (and perhaps also 'signed English'). Now, they must take on board a new medium, computer-mediated English, where many of the expectations and practices which we associate with spoken and written language no longer obtain.

We need a name for this new medium, and over a dozen have been proposed, such as 'computer-mediated communication' and 'electronic discourse'. A firm believer in the succinct, I call it *Netspeak*. If you want to focus exclusively on English, you may find *Netlish* convenient. I am comfortable with Netspeak, for it falls within a tradition of usage which began with George Orwell's *Newspeak* and *Oldspeak* in *1984*, later developments such as *Airspeak* and *Seaspeak*, and media labels such as *Royalspeak* and *Blairspeak*. It is functional enough, as long as we remember that 'speak' here involves writing as well as talking, and that any 'speak' suffix also has a receptive element, including 'listening and reading'.

Before I go into the nature of English Netspeak, it is worth stressing the point that it is a medium, not a variety. To see this, think of radio broadcasting. It doesn't make sense to talk about radio broadcasting as a 'variety' of English; rather, it is a more abstract notion – a medium, or channel – which is represented by many linguistically distinctive varieties – newsreading, weather-forecasting, sports commentary, monologue talks, plays, and so on. Some of these varieties consist, in turn, of sub-varieties – think of all the kinds of sports commentary, for instance, and how different they are linguistically (football, cricket, snooker, horse-racing, tennis ...). Netspeak, likewise, is a medium, consisting of many varieties, some of which in turn consist of several sub-varieties. I came to this conclusion after researching my book, *Language and the Internet* (2001). Within the Net, I was able to find five main domains within which varieties of Netspeak could be identified – there is the World Wide Web, e-mail, two types of chatgroup (the synchronous type, which operate in real-time, and the asynchronous type, where you leave a message in an electronic location and hope someone will read it one day), and the domain of virtual worlds, where you role-play imaginary situations in long-running games for edification or just plain fun. I am in no doubt that this figure of five is soon going to grow as new technologies come to be; but these are the five that are out there right now.

The crucial point is to recognize the way a technology directly shapes a form of linguistic expression. The history of writing repeatedly shows how a new technology (the cuneiform wedge, for instance) can literally give shape to language. Printing did the same, as did the telegraph, typewriter, telegram, and other technologies up to and including the latest, texting – the short-messaging service where the small screen size immediately motivated an unprecedented range of abbreviated linguistic expression. It is the same with computer-mediated communication, as seen in the Internet, where the technology has enabled a whole new medium of communication to come into being, something that is electronic, global and interactive, and this has given rise to a distinctive type of language, neither spoken nor written.

It is not like writing, firstly, because it lacks one of the most basic features of traditional writing – the fact that a piece of text is static and permanent on the page. If something is written down, repeated reference to it will be an encounter with an unchanged text. We would be surprised if, upon returning to a particular page, it had altered its graphic character in some way. Putting it like this, we can see immediately that Netspeak is not by any means like conventional writing. A 'page' on the Web often varies from encounter to encounter (and all have the option of varying, even if page-owners choose not to take it) for several possible reasons: its factual content might have been updated, its advertising sponsor might have changed, or its graphic designer might have added new features. Nor is the writing that you see necessarily static, given the technical options available which allow text to move around the screen, disappear/reappear, change colour, and so on. From a user point of view, there are opportunities to 'interfere' with the text in all kinds of ways that are not possible in traditional writing. A page, once downloaded to the user's screen, may have its text cut, added to, revised, annotated, even totally restructured, in ways that make the result seem to come from the same source as the original. E-mails too are variable: we may delete them, edit them, cut and paste in them, all with an ease and undetectability that is not possible when people try to alter a traditionally written text.

But Netspeak is not like speech either, because it lacks the kind of simultaneous feedback you get in face-to-face conversation, or the immediate reaction signals which people make to each other (the *mhms* and nods). When you are sending me a message I cannot react to it while you are writing it, because until it arrives on my screen I have no idea that it exists. And when it does arrive, there is a delay before I can give you a response, which makes the rhythm of the exchange totally unlike that of conversation. Nor is Netspeak like speech, in that there is no way of expressing the full range of vocal variations in pitch (intonation), loudness (stress), speed, rhythm, pause, and tone of voice. As with traditional writing, of course, there have been somewhat desperate efforts to capture these effects in the form of an exaggerated use of spelling and punctuation, and the use of capitals, spacing, and special symbols for emphasis. Examples include repeated letters (*aaaaahhhhh, hiiiiiii, ooops, soooo*), repeated punctuation marks (*no more!!!!!, whohe????, hey!!!!!!!!!, see what you started??????????????????*), and a range of emphatic conventions:

all capitals for 'shouting'	I SAID NO
letter spacing for 'loud and clear'	W H Y N O T, w h y n o t
word/phrase emphasis by asterisks	the * real * answer

These features are certainly capable of a certain expressiveness, but the range of meanings they signal is few, and restricted to gross notions such as extra emphasis, surprise, and puzzlement.

Related to this is the way Netspeak lacks the facial expressions, gestures, and conventions of body posture and distance which are so critical in expressing personal opinions and attitudes and in moderating social relationships. The limitation was noted early in the development of Netspeak, and led to the introduction of *smileys* or *emoticons*. These are combinations of keyboard characters designed to show an emotional facial expression: they are typed in sequence on a single line, and placed after the final punctuation mark of a sentence. Almost all of them are read sideways. The two basic types

:-) or :)   :-(or : (

express positive attitudes and negative attitudes respectively (the omission of the 'nose' element seems to be solely a function of typing speed or personal taste). It is plain that they are an extremely crude way of capturing some of the basic features of facial expression, and their semantic role is limited. In fact, they are not especially frequent; in one study, only 13% of 3,000 posts contained them – and many people do not use them at all.

Netspeak is not like speech or writing. It is not a hybrid of spoken and written features. It does things that neither of these other mediums could ever do, and must accordingly be seen as a new species of communication. My own vision of Netspeak is of something genuinely different in kind. Electronic texts are simply not the same as other kinds of texts. In particular, they display a dynamism that is lacking elsewhere, in the way texts can be manipulated and changed. And they permit a multiplicity of simultaneous communicative activities that neither speech nor writing could tolerate – such as hypertext links between documents or carrying on half-a-dozen conversations at the same time with other members of a chatroom. This is why I talk of Netspeak as a genuine 'third medium'. I do believe it is a revolutionary moment, in the history of language. 50–100,000 years ago, speech. 8–10,000 years ago, writing. And now, computer-mediated language.

How far have people begun to develop an intuition that varieties of Netspeak exist? The fact that people are conscious of something 'out there' is demonstrated by the way other varieties of language are being affected by it. It is always a sure sign that a new variety has 'arrived' when people in other linguistic situations start alluding to it. In everyday conversation, terms from the underlying computer technology are given a new application among people who want their talk to have a cool cutting-edge. So I am impressed when I hear such examples as these:

- It's my turn to download now (i.e. I've heard all your gossip, now hear mine)
- I need more bandwidth to handle that point (i.e. I can't take it all in at once)
- She's multitasking (said of someone doing two things at once)
- Let's go offline for a few minutes (i.e. let's talk in private)
- Give me a brain dump on that (i.e. tell me all you know)
- Are you wired? (i.e. ready to handle this)
- Get with the programme (i.e. keep up)
- I got a pile of spam in the post today (i.e. junk-mail)
- E you later (said as a farewell).

Let's look at a couple of examples in more detail. *Dot com* is now a commonly heard phrase, as well as appearing ubiquitously in writing in all kinds of advertising and promotional material. But written English shows developments well beyond the stage of the literal use of *.com*. It has come to be used as a general adjective (with or without the period, and sometimes hyphenated), as in *dotcom organizations* and *dotcom crisis*. It has also come to be used in a variety of ludic ways, especially in those varieties where language play is a dominant motif – newspaper headlines and advertising. The similarity of *com* to *come* has been noticed: an offer to win a car on the Internet is headed *.com and get it*. A headline in the *Independent Graduate* on openings still available on the Web is headed: *Dot.com all ye faithful*. A phonetic similarity motivated a food-outlet advertisement: *lunch@Boots.yum*. The 'dot' element is now introduced into all kinds of phrases: *Learnhow.to* and *launch.anything* are names of sites. *un.complicated* introduced an ad for personal finance. One company uses the slogan *Get around the www.orld;* another has the slogan *www.alk this way*.

A similar ludic trend applies to the symbol @, now the universal link between recipient and address. It was chosen pragmatically by a computer engineer, Ray Tomlinson, who sent the first network e-mail in 1972. He needed a character which did not occur in names, and this typewriter keyboard symbol stood out, with the bonus of having an appropriate meaning (of someone being 'at' somewhere). A subsequent irony is that many firms and organizations have replaced the letter *a* or *at* in their name by an @, as in @tractions, @cafe, @Home, @pex. And it has been seen turning up in other settings where traditionally the word *at* would be used: *This is where it's* @ is one slogan; Bill

Gates' 1999 book is called *Business @ the speed of thought.* It has even been added to text where the word *at* would not normally appear: a postcard to my house read: *Crystals* @ ... followed by the address.

The *e-* prefix is another index of Netspeak's influence. By now it has been used in hundreds of expressions. *The Oxford Dictionary of New Words* (1997) had already noted *e-text*, *e-zine*, *e-cash*, and *e-money*, and in 1998 the American Dialect Society named *e-* 'Word [sic] of the Year' as well as 'Most Useful and Most Likely to Succeed'. Examples since noted include *e-tailing* and *e-tailers* ['retailing on the Internet'], *e-lance* ['electronic free-lance'] and *e-lancers*, *e-therapy* and *e-therapists*, *e-management* and *e-managers*, *e-government*, *e-bandwagon*, *e-books*, *e-conferences*, *e-voting*, *e-loan*, *e-newsletters*, *e-security*, *e-cards*, *e-pinions*, *e-shop*, *e-list*, *e-rage*, and *e-crap*. A bookmaker developing a Net presence called the firm *e-we go*.

How many of these developments will become a permanent feature of the language it is impossible to say. There are already signs of a reaction against some of the above usages. A Silicon Valley company, Persistence Software, is reported to be campaigning against the proliferation of e-words: it has established The Society for the Preservation of the Other 25 Letters of the Alphabet. But this only makes the general hypothesis more compelling, that a notion of Netspeak has begun to evolve which is rapidly becoming a part of popular linguistic consciousness, and evoking strong language attitudes. The problem, from an ELT point of view, is of course that English speakers are still getting to grips with the communicative potential made available to them. They are in a learning situation of a rather special kind. They are having to acquire the rules (of how to communicate via e-mail, of how to talk in chatgroups, of how to construct an effective Web page, and so on), and yet there are no rules, in the sense of universally agreed modes of behaviour established by generations of usage. Teachers don't like the sound of that: if there are no rules, how can we teach them? There is a clear contrast with the familiar world of paper-based communication. Letter-writing, for instance, is routinely taught in school; and because there is widespread agreement on how letters are to be written, supported by the recommendations of usage manuals, we feel secure in that knowledge. We know such conventions as how to use opening and closing formulae (*Dear Sir/Madam, Yours faithfully*), where to put the address and date, and how to break up the text into paragraphs. Adults make use of this knowledge almost without thinking, and on occasion, as in informal letter-writing, they dare to break the rules with confidence. But with the Internet equivalent of letter-writing – e-mails – there is no such long tradition. Most people have been using e-mails for less than a decade, and they are unaware of the factors which have to be respected if their messages are not to be misunderstood. Often, the first indication that they have misconstructed a message comes when they receive an unpalatable response from the recipient.

A big difficulty, from the teaching point of view, is that a strong personal, creative spirit imbues Netspeak, as an emerging medium. The rate at which users have been coining new terms and introducing playful variations into established words has no parallel in contemporary language use. The *Jargon File*, which records 'the language hackers use among themselves for fun, social communication, and technical debate', is quite clear about its innovative, ludic, dynamic properties: 'Hackers ... regard slang formation and use as a game to be played for conscious pleasure'. We respond to 'the voice of the quirky, individualistic writer', say the authors of *Wired Style*, in expounding one of their principles, and they recommend: 'play with voice'.

You have to be careful if you consult these guides, because they are reflecting a stage in the development of Netspeak which is already changing. As hackers built the Internet and gave physical presence to its various situations, they have naturally developed a sense of ownership of Netspeak which is reflected in the attitudes of the current generation of dictionaries and style guides. But the beast they have created is now so large that it is beyond ownership. The hacker community is but a tiny part of the online population, and the linguistic intuitions and preferences of such vast numbers are immensely variable and impossible to control. Quirky, individualistic writers there will be among them; but there will also be huge numbers of non-quirky, conservative writers, who don't go in for wordplay. The future of Netspeak, then, is very much bound up with the extent to which hacker-originated language and style has developed a sufficiently stable and powerful identity to motivate new Internet users to use it, or whether these users will introduce fresh linguistic directions, evolving norms of stylistic usage which owe nothing to hacker origins, and which avoid the playful and esoteric features so much in evidence now. The evidence suggests that it is the second direction which is the dominant contemporary trend.

Publications such as *Wired Style* have their place as part of a climate of opinion which will eventually help to shape Netspeak. The principles are important statements, as they make explicit a set of intuitions about language which are likely to be influential. Under one of their principles, 'Anticipating the future', they include such 'style commandments' as 'Save a keystroke' and 'When in doubt, close it up'. The former is illustrated by the replacement of initial capital letters by lower-case letters – as in *webmaster* and *telnet*. The latter refers to the trend for originally spaced compound words to become hyphenated and then written solid (as in such everyday examples as *flower pot*, *flower-pot*, and *flowerpot*). The authors are well aware that this is a regular feature of linguistic change, and they are keen to hasten the process: 'Go there now.' They recommend *startup*, *homepage*, and *email*, for example. 'The way of the Net is just not a hyphenated way.' Comments of this kind are bound to influence people (such as myself) who have no idea what is normal usage, in Internet situations. I have always spelled *e-mail* with a hyphen, and have done so in my book. Whether I change to *email* in due course will depend on whether a consensus emerges. I have no aesthetic axe to grind, and the presence of the additional keystroke is not going to have a serious effect upon my life. Eventually, one standard of usage will prevail, and it will probably be the solid form. In the meantime, it is important to recognize the fact that there is a great deal of divided usage in Netspeak, and to treat with caution those guides which come down on one side or the other.

So what are the distinctive linguistic features of Netspeak? They are to be found under two main headings: the lexicon and the graphology. A large number of words and phrases have emerged which are needed to talk about Internet-restricted situations, operations, activities and personnel, making this one of the most creative lexical domains in contemporary English, involving all major lexical processes. Many terms are associated with the software which enables people to use the Internet, and which routinely appear on screen. Some have a permanent presence (albeit in hidden menus), in the form of the labels used to designate screen areas and functions, and to specify user options and commands (*file, edit, view, insert, paste, format, tools, help, save*). Some terms appear only at intervals on a screen, depending on circumstances – usually, when things are going wrong, in the form of error messages (*illegal operation, error, not found* – there seem to be no positive messages to tell us that everything is going right). Several terms are associated with the use of computer hardware (*freeze, lock, down, hang, crash, bomb, client* [the machine, not the user]). And terms have emerged for the population of Internet users themselves (*netizens, netters, netties, netheads, cybersurfers, nerds, newbies*).

A popular method of creating Internet neologisms is to combine two separate words to make a new word, or *compound*. Some elements turn up repeatedly: *mouse* in such forms as *mouseclick, mousepad, mouse across, mouse over*; *click* in *click-and-buy, one-click, cost-per-click, double click*; *ware* in *firmware, freeware, groupware, shareware, shovelware, wetware* ['brain']; *web* in *webcam, webmail, webliography, webmaster, webzine, webhead* ['Web addict']; *net* in *netlag, netdead, netnews, hypernet, Usenet, Netspeak, EcoNet, PeaceNet*; *hot* in *hotlist, hotspot, hotlink, Hotmail, HotBot, HotJava*; and *bug* ['software error'] in *bug fix, bugtracker, bug bash* ['hunt for bugs'], *BugNet*. Similar in function are the use of *cyber-* and *hyper-* as prefixes or combining forms (*cyberspace, cyberculture, cyberlawyer, cybersex, cyber rights*; *hypertext, hyperlink, hyperfiction, hyperzine*) and the suffixal use of *-bot* [an artificial intelligence program, from *robot*], as in *annoybot, chatterbot, knowbot, cancelbot, softbot, mailbot, spybot*. Other prefixes include *e-* (already illustrated); *V-* ['virtual'], and *E* [for a number raised to a power, from mathematics], as in *V-chat* ['virtual chat'], *ThanksE6* ['Thanks a million']. The word *at*, often shown as @, also has an increasingly prefixal function, as in *atcommand, atsign, @-party, @-address*. Blends (in which part of one word is joined to part of another) are illustrated by *netiquette, netizen, infonet, datagram, infobahn, Internaut, Bugzilla* [a bug-tracking agency]. An innovation is the replacement of a word-element by a similar sounding item, as we have already seen in the use of *e-* (*ecruiting* ['electronic recruiting'], *ecruiter, etailing* ['electronic retailing']). Another is the retaining of the period found in electronic addresses within certain compounds, as a kind of infix, seen in *net.legend, net.abuse, net.police, net.citizen*, with the punctuation mark often spoken aloud as 'dot'. In a development which will cause delight to all Anglo-Saxonists, the *-en* plural of *oxen* is found with some words ending in *-x*, such as *boxen, vaxen* ['VAX computers'], *matrixen, bixen* ['users of BIX', an information exchange system] – a usage which could well increase, given that so many computing names end in *-X*. Word-class conversion is important, too, usually from noun to verb, as in *to mouse, to clipboard, to geek out* ['talk technically'], *to 404* ['be unable to find a page'].

The various types of abbreviation found in Netspeak have been one of its most remarked features. A tiny sample would include *BBS* ['bulletin board system'], *BCC* ['blind carbon copy'], *DNS* ['domain name system'], *FAQ* ['frequently asked question'], *HTML* ['hypertext markup language'], *ISP* ['Internet Service Provider'], *URL* ['uniform resource locator'], and the names of many firms and sites, such as *AOL, IBM, IRC*. Letter-plus-number combinations are also found: *W3C* ['World Wide Web Consortium'], *3Com* [a data-networking organization], *P3P* ['Platform for Privacy Preferences'], *Go2Net*. Newer technology, such as the WAP-phones ['Wireless Application Protocol'] with their tiny screens, have motivated a whole new genre of abbreviated forms. The acronyms are no longer restricted to words or short phrases, but can be sentence-length, as in *AYSOS* ['Are you stupid or something?'], *CID* ['Consider it done'], *CIO* ['Check it out'], *GTG* ['Got to go'], *WDYS* ['What did you say?']. Individual words can be reduced to two or three letters: *PLS* ['please'], *THX* or *TX* ['thanks'], *WE* ['whatever']. Some are like rebuses, in that the sound value of the letter or numeral acts as a syllable of a word, or are combinations of rebus and letter initial: *B4N* ['Bye For Now'], *CYL* ['See you later'], *L8R* ['later']. There are dictionaries of such forms now.

Distinctive graphology is also an important feature of Netspeak. The range extends from an enhanced system (by comparison with traditional writing) with a wide range of special fonts and styles, as in the most sophisticated Web pages, to a severely reduced system, with virtually no typographic contrastivity (not even such 'basic' features as italics or boldface), as in many e-mails and chatgroup conversations. All orthographic features have been affected. For example, the status of capitalization varies greatly. Most of the Internet is not case-sensitive, which thus motivates the random use of capitals or no capitals at all. There is a strong tendency to use lower-case everywhere. The 'save a keystroke' principle is widely found, where whole sentences can be produced without capitals (or punctuation): *john are you going to london next week*. The lower-case default mentality means that any use of capitalization is a strongly marked form of communication. Messages wholly in capitals are considered to be 'shouting', and usually avoided; words in capitals add extra emphasis (with asterisks and spacing also available), as already illustrated. There are, however, certain contexts where capitals need to be recognized. A capital letter may be obligatory in a business name (especially if trade-marked). Indeed, a distinctive feature of Internet graphology is the way two capitals are used – one initial, one medial – a phenomenon variously called *bicapitalization* (*BiCaps*), *intercaps*, *incaps*, and *midcaps*: *AltaVista, RetrievalWare, ScienceDirect, ThomsonDirect, NorthernLight, PostScript, PowerBook, DreamWorks, GeoCities, EarthLink, PeaceNet, SportsZone, HotWired, CompuServe, AskJeeves*. More complex examples include *QuarkXPress, aRMadillo Online*.

Spelling practice is also distinctive. In English, US spelling is more common than British, partly for historical reasons (the origins of the Internet), and partly for reasons of economy, most US spellings being a character shorter than British ones (*color* vs *colour*, etc). New spelling conventions have emerged, such as the replacement of plural *-s* by *-z* to refer to pirated versions of software, as in *warez, tunez, gamez, serialz, pornz, downloadz, filez*. Nonstandard spelling, heavily penalized in traditional writing (at least, since the eighteenth century), is used without sanction in conversational settings. Spelling errors in an e-mail would not be assumed to be an indication of lack of education (though they may be) but purely a function of typing inaccuracy. Nonstandard spellings are used to reflect pronunciation, such as *yep, yup, yay, nope, noooo, kay* ('OK'), *sokay* ['It's OK']. Emotional expressions of horror, shock, and the like make use of varying numbers of vowels and consonants, depending on the ferocity of the emotion: *aaaiiieee, yayyyyyyy*. Some deviant spellings have become so widely used as to be virtually standard in this variety, such as *phreak, phreaker, phreaking* [= 'freak', etc]. Some are still restricted to certain groups of users, such as the *-y-* spelling (from *byte*) introduced into certain expressions for bit blocks of different sizes: *tayste, tydbit* (2 bits), *nybble* (4 bits), *playte* (16 bits), *dynner* (32 bits). The dollar sign sometimes replaces *S*, if some sort of dig is being made about costs, as in *Micro$oft*, and a £ sign can replace *L*, as in *AO£*. Teenage users, in particular, have introduced several deviant spellings, such as *kool*, *c%l* ['cool'], *fone* ['phone'], *d00dz* ['dudes'], *l0zers* ['losers']. Among this group of users, the *k* is often used as an emphatic prefix, producing such forms as *k-kool*, *k-awesome*, *k-k-allright*.

Punctuation tends to be minimalist in most situations, and completely absent in some e-mails and chat exchanges. It is an important area, for it is the chief means a language has for bringing writing into direct contact with (the prosody of) speech, as well as conveying a great deal of information about grammatical construction. A lot depends on personality: some e-mailers are scrupulous about maintaining a traditional punctuation; others use it when they have to, to avoid ambiguity; and some do not use it at all, either as a consequence of typing speed, or through not realizing that ambiguity can be one of the consequences. On the other hand, there is an increased use of symbols not normally part of the traditional punctuation system, such as the hash: #. Unusual combinations of punctuation marks can occur, such as (to express pause): ....., —, and ,,,,,. Emphasis and attitude can result in exaggerated or random use of punctuation, such as *!!!!!!!* or *£$£$%!*. A potential contrastivity seems to be emerging, in the use of some pairs, notably the scope of emphasis indicated by the asterisk. The two sentences below convey rather different effects: the second is much slower and more emphatic.

This is a * very * important point.
This is a * very * * important * * point.*

However, the asterisk is still developing a range of functions, and is at times used somewhat idiosyncratically.

The most general features of Netspeak distinctiveness are currently found chiefly in graphology and the lexicon – the levels of language where it is relatively easy to introduce innovation and deviation. As with language change in general, grammatical variation is less frequent or widespread. When it does occur it tends to be restricted to a particular situation or group of users. For example, the phenomenon of *verb reduplication* occurs in some chatgroups, and occasionally elsewhere, but as yet is not a universally encountered feature. A verb (from a fairly small set) is used twice in immediate succession to express a range of functions, such as an expression of pleasure or pain, as a sarcastic or exasperated reaction, or simply as a turn-marking marker, showing that an utterance is ended:

How about that! Win, win. ['the program has performed successfully']
I deleted your message. Lose, lose! ['I'm stupid']

So far I have been illustrating features which can be found across Netspeak domains. When we examine a particular domain in greater detail, there is evidence of further linguistic distinctiveness. I shall use some features of e-mails to illustrate the point. E-mails have a fixed internal structure, and each element of that structure has its conventions. For instance, in the body of an e-mail, there are both obligatory and optional elements. The obligatory item is, patently, a message of some sort. What is interesting is the extent to which it is preceded by a *greeting* (or *salutation*, *opening*) and followed by a *farewell* (or *signature*, *closing*). Several types of e-mail have no greeting at all. They include first messages from people who do not know the recipient, and are therefore typical in the case of public announcements and junk-mail. Some messages include an automatically derived 'Dear X' or 'Hi, X' to their openings, often with bizarre results. Automatic junk-greetings in my case have included *Hi, Professor D; Hello, Crystal; Dear Mr Wales.*

Between people who know each other, greetingless messages are usually promptly sent responses, where the responder sees the message as the second part of a two-part interaction (an *adjacency pair*), for which an introductory greeting is inappropriate. For example (a) is all right, but (b) would be unlikely, and (c) even less so.

Arriving message: David, will 7.30 be OK for the talk? Colin
(a) Response message: Fine
(b) Response message: *Colin, Fine.
(c) Response message: *Dear Colin,
Fine.

The longer the delay in responding, the more likely the response will contain a greeting, if only an apology for the time-lag.

By contrast, two-thirds of a sample of 500 e-mails in my Deleted folder from people who know me contained an introductory greeting.

- *–Dear*
- General word: *Hi, Hello again, Hi there!, Bonjour*
- General word plus ID: *Hi from Pete, Goodday from Oz*
- Intimate name alone: *David, david, Dave, DC, Dad*
- Combination of general word and intimate name: *Hi David, Hey D, Hello David, Hello DC, Good morning David, Howdy David, Hi dad*
- Formal name: *Professor Crystal, Professor*
- [but never (yet): General word and formal name: **Hi, Professor Crystal, *Hello Professor*]
- *+Dear*
- With intimate name: *Dear David, Dear Dave*
- With whole name: *Dear David Crystal, Annwyl David Crystal* [Welsh: 'Dear']
- With title and surname: *Dear Professor Crystal, Dear Dr Crystal, Dear Mr Crystal, Estimado profesor Crystal*

They express a wide range of effects, from most formal to most informal, and indicate several kinds of social relationship and intimacy. They could be classified in many ways, but an important variable is the use of an initial endearment (*+Dear* messages were twice as common as *–Dear* messages). By far the most frequent individual greeting formula was *Dear David*, followed by *David*, then *Hi David*, confirming the general view about the medium as a means of informal interaction between people who know each other.

Farewells display fewer possibilities for variation, but the same points of principle arise. Two elements are available: a pre-closing formula (of the *Best wishes* type) and the identification of the sender. Most interpersonal messages (80% in my case) end with both elements present, and the influence of traditional letter-writing is evident in the overwhelming tendency to place each element on a separate line, usually spaced away from the message body. The remaining 20% give a name, and dispense with the formula.

The usual range of formulae, known from traditional letter-writing, is employed, with the same range of functions (affection, gratitude, expectation, communicative intent, and so on): *Lots of love, Thanks for everything, See you soon, Let me know if this isn't clear* .... The informality of the medium is reflected in the relative absence of the *Yours sincerely* type (turning up in only 5% of my messages, though it seems to be increasing). There seems to be no difference between old and young in their predilection for formulae, though preferences vary dramatically, as we would expect. (I cannot see myself ever using *ta-ta, babe* used by one of my children to her friend. Sadly, I don't seem to know any 'babes'.)

The overriding impression I have, even from such a small sample of material, is of the remarkable amount of variation which is found within the medium. E-mail guidebooks present a much more standardized picture, and in their prescriptions reduce the range of options quite considerably. One of them is unequivocal in its support for first-name only: 'Start the message with the person's first name if you're communicating with a person you know on that basis'. However, as with other domains, such as letter-writing, having a range of linguistic options increases the communicative power of a medium, and usage manuals need to recognize this. In any case, people are voting with their feet: as e-mail becomes a routine part of social life, at all levels, it will inevitably be influenced by the linguistic practices of its users. Already many people use it as a more immediate and practical way of sending formal letters and greetings cards. In recent months I have received official invitations, letters of agreement, and many other formal communications through this medium, and replied to them in the same way. It is likely that the technological benefits of the medium (in terms of speed, forwarding, automatic typesetting, etc.) will eventually be a more important driving force than the fact that it permits a greater degree of informal communication than existed before. My prediction is therefore that e-mail in a few years' time will display a much wider stylistic range than it does at present, as the medium is adapted to suit a broader range of communicative purposes, and the legal issues surrounding the status of certain types of message come to be resolved.

The clarity of the message on the screen is a dominant theme of e-mail manuals. Clarity in this context involves both legibility and intelligibility. Legibility chiefly refers to ways of avoiding a screenful of unbroken text. Writers are recommended to use a line-of-white between paragraphs, for example, or to highlight points in a list using a bullet or numbering facility. (The increased use of bullet points is an important stylistic feature of e-mails, having previously been rare in letters and typewritten documents.) They are advised to use short, simple sentences, long ones being felt to be more difficult to read on screen. But all questions of legibility have to be considered from two points of view – the reader's as well as the writer's. This is one of the unique features of e-mail communication: there is no guarantee that the message as reproduced on the writer's screen will appear in the same configuration when it reaches the reader's. A common problem is for the line-length settings to differ, so that a message which sat neatly in 100-character lines at the sender's terminal is reproduced with a highly erratic sequence of long and short line-lengths on the receiving screen, or fails to wrap around at all (requiring an awkward repeated right-scrolling manoeuvre), or is processed so that the end part of each line is simply left out. In addition, any special formatting (such as the use of bold or italic typefaces) may be lost in transmission. And attachments may be unreadable at the other end. No other type of written communication presents us with such potential asymmetry.

The pressure to maintain a message's intelligibility might be thought to be no different from that encountered in any other communicative domain. But the speed and spontaneity with which e-mails can be written and sent makes it more likely that the processes of reflection normally used with written language will not take place. Evidently many people do not read through their message before sending it – often with the unintended consequence that the first reply they receive is a request for clarification. Misspellings, for example, are a natural feature of the body message in an e-mail. They occur, regardless of the educational background of the writer, in any situation where there is fast typing and a lack of editorial revision. For the most part, these errors cause little or no disruption to the communicative process. No-one is likely to be misled by such e-lines as:

I'll procede with the practical arrangments.
Hav eyou got the tikcets yet?

Nor is the reader going to make a social judgement about the writer's educational ability, on the basis of such data – a contrast with what *would* happen if someone wrote a traditional letter containing such errors. Of the hundreds of e-mail typing errors I have seen, hardly any really interfere with the meaning. Nonetheless, some manuals are hotly against misspellings of any kind. And the same anxiety is expressed over omitted capitalization and punctuation. The attitude doubtless has some force in the context of business communication, where prescriptive attitudes are likely to be strongly present, consciously or unconsciously. But as a principle of general guidance for all e-mail users, it is unreal. Lightly punctuated and uncapitalized messages, given the relatively short sentence lengths, pose few problems of ambiguity:

log onto the address below and you will see a mock up of our site
this is an excerpt from a tommy cooper story i got

More important, in relation to intelligibility, is the question of a message's coherence, arising out of the inherently dialogic character of e-messaging. Although some e-mails are sent without any expectation of a response, the vast majority do expect a reply – and get one. Accordingly, the communicative unit, as in everyday conversation, is the *exchange*. The chief linguistic evidence for exchanges is the frequency with which response messages begin with an acknowledgement that there has been a previous message: direct feedback expressions, just as in everyday conversation, or elliptical and anaphoric (referring-back) devices, as the queries illustrate in this selection of opening sentences:

Yes, I think you're right [about what?]
No, he won't be there [who? where?].

An explicit acknowledgement of the existence of a previous message is common: excluding replies which have been automatically generated (usually because the recipient is away), 70% of my messages begin with an acknowledgement, as in:

Thanks for your message
Many thanks for your thoughts
Sorry for the delay in replying

Formality varies greatly: *Thank you, Thanks, THX, Ta* .... In my corpus, the majority of the messages *without* any acknowledgement were very short – often one line or one word in length. This is understandable: it would be anomalous to add an acknowledgement which would be longer than the meat of the response. The following seems highly unlikely:

?*Thanks for your message. Yes.

Acknowledgement is also sometimes omitted when the full text of the previous message is reproduced further down the screen, as when use has been made of the 'Reply to Author' option. The opposite situation also occurs, with a reply message consisting solely of an acknowledgement, such as *Thanks*. Usage manuals differ in their views about this practice: some warm to the fact that a courtesy has been expressed; others castigate it as a time-wasting device.

The dialogic character of the body element in an e-mail is made totally explicit when the 'Reply to Author' option is activated, and respondents add reactions which refer directly to the whole of a received message. The process is facilitated by the software, which makes a clear typographic distinction between original message and reaction. After early experiments using indention, standard practice is now to insert a right-pointing angle bracket (sometimes a colon or vertical black line) at the beginning of each line of the original message (including the paragraph-separating lines-of-white), so that (a) becomes (b).

(a) I hope to be there by six, though everything depends on the trains. Will you be coming by train yourself, or are you driving this time? I know Fred is bringing his car ...

(b) >I hope to be there by six, though everything depends on the trains. Will
>you be coming by train yourself, or are you driving this time? I know
>Fred is bringing his car ...

The reaction may then be added, in any of three locations: above the whole of the received message, below it, or within it – repeatedly, if necessary. The procedure is a little like adding notes at the beginning or end of a letter, or in the margins, and returning it to the sender – but with the difference that in e-mail both parties end up with a perfect copy of everything.

It is the within-message comment which is really interesting, from a linguistic point of view. This is especially used when several points are being made which require individual attention. A within-message reply to (a) above might read as in (c):

(c) >I hope to be there by six, though everything depends on the trains.
I know – remember last time?
>Will you be coming by train yourself, or are you driving this time?
Car
>I know Fred is bringing his car ...

It would not be intelligible to give the sequence of responses illustrated in (d) at the end of the message, or as in (e) at the beginning.

(d) >I hope to be there by six, though everything depends on the trains. Will
>you be coming by train yourself, or are you driving this time? I know
>Fred is bringing his car.
I know – remember last time?
Car

(e) I know – remember last time?
Car
>I hope to be there by six, though everything depends on the trains. Will
>you be coming by train yourself, or are you driving this time? I know
>Fred is bringing his car.

To make either intelligible would require major rewriting, with more explicit cross-reference to or paraphrasing of what the sender had said. In business communication, where documents can be very long and reactions to individual points erratically located, guidebook advice to avoid within-message reactions is well-taken. A point might easily be missed, and it would be difficult to work out the nature of the overall reply from a sequence of individual, widely separated reactions.

Message intercalation is a unique feature of e-mail language, and a property which could only succeed in an electronic medium. And there is a further refinement. It is possible for recipients to respond to an original message not by adding reactions to selected parts of the original text, but by editing the original text so that only those parts which require reaction are left. The procedure is, effectively, one of quotation. Thus, for example, I sent the following paragraph (a) to someone, who replied as (b), cutting one of my sentences and pasting it into the new message.

(a) There are still several loose ends for the Tuesday. We've had a lot of people wanting to contribute, and our original proposals for timing seem to be out. Do you think it would work having two sessions in the afternoon? It would mean cutting down on the tea-break, and maybe even timing dinner a half-hour later than usual. That in turn would push the evening session on a bit, but I don't see any problem there, as everyone is staying the night.

(b) >Do you think it would work having two sessions in the afternoon?
Good idea

The longer a sender's paragraphs, the more likely the recipient is to respond in this way. The result has been described as *framing*, because of the way in which the quoted text is demarcated typographically, either through an angle-bracket or a vertical line. Framing is a consequence of the ease with which people can cut and paste from an original message.

Framing has both strengths and weaknesses. It is a convenience, in that a series of points can be responded to rapidly and succinctly, either in the order in which they were made or in some fresh order – much as we can strategically recapitulate a series of points made by an interlocutor in a face-to-face discussion. Time and memory are saved, as it is no longer necessary to trawl back through an e-mail thread to find the original remarks. And dealing with several points at once saves repeated e-mailing. Reactions to reactions are also possible, with each new reaction retaining its own framing device, so that the page takes on a nested appearance, as shown by the increasing angle brackets in:

>B's extract from A's message
>>A's extract from B's message
>>>B's extract from A's extract ...

On the other hand, everybody knows the difficulties which arise when quotations are being used extensively: meaning can change dramatically when words are quoted out of context, whether innocently or deliberately. Deliberate out-of-context quotation may seem a strange concept to people expecting the e-mail or chatgroup worlds to be inhabited by polite, well-mannered individuals. But misquotation, in order to score a point, is widespread.

A framed message is certainly a most unusual object, not like anything else in language use. The stylistic consequences of cutting and pasting text from an earlier message – either our own or someone else's – are also unusual; here, too, there is nothing remotely like it in other domains of writing. Where else would we find so much physically adjacent but semantically unrelated paragraphs of text? In traditional writing, such texts would be penalized for lack of organization and logical progression; but in an e-mail, where the points are taking up different issues in a previous message, such overriding considerations are waived. The bottom line is that, with e-mail, a new document is created with every transaction. The permanence of e-writing is only a superficial impression. Although a single piece of text may be preserved throughout a thread of messages, via forwarding or replying to author, each screen incarnation gives it a different status and may present it in a different form – either through electronic interference from the software or editorial interference from the new user.

Writers repeatedly draw analogies between e-mail and other forms of communication, in order to locate it in communicative 'space'. Homer Simpson has it explained to him in this way:

Homer: What's an e-mail?
Lenny: It's a computer thing, like, er, an electric letter.
Carl: Or a quiet phone call.

From the above analysis, it is clear that e-mails do indeed have elements of the memo about them, notably in their fixed header structure. The informal letter analogy is also appropriate, with the medium's reliance on greetings and farewells, and the use of several informal written features in the message body. The telephone conversation analogy is also proper, given the way a dialogue style can build up over time; and the cheapness of the medium has often been remarked. And some e-mails are highly telegrammatic in style. But e-mail, in the final analysis, is like none of these. It is not written speech nor spoken writing. It is, formally and functionally, unique.

The evolution of e-mail style is in its infancy, and perhaps the only thing we can say for certain is that it will soon no longer be as it currently is. Generalizations about the medium have hitherto been heavily influenced by its technical origins and early years of use. There is an understandable tendency to think of e-mailing solely in terms of informality. It feels temporary, indeed, and this promotes a sense of the carefree. Messages can be easily deleted, which suggests that their content is basically unimportant. Because of its spontaneity, speed, privacy and leisure value, e-mail offers the option of greater levels of informality than are found elsewhere in traditional writing. But as the medium matures, it is becoming apparent that it is not exclusively an informal medium, and received opinion is going to have to change. The result will be a medium which will portray a wide range of stylistic expressiveness, from formal to informal, just as other mediums have come to do, and where the pressure on users will be to display stylistic consistency, in the same way that this is required in other forms of writing. E-mail will then take its place in the school curriculum, not as a medium to be feared for its linguistic irresponsibility (because it allows radical graphological deviance) but as one which offers a further domain within which children can develop their ability to consolidate their stylistic intuitions and make responsible linguistic choices. E-mail has extended the language's stylistic range in interesting and motivating ways. In my view, it is an opportunity, not a threat, for language education.

I am therefore very supportive of the various initiatives to introduce e-mail and other Internet domains into the ELT world. David Eastment, for example, carried out a survey on English-language teaching (ELT) in relation to the Internet, on behalf of the British Council in 1996, and was in 'no doubt that the Internet ... will eventually transform the way that the teaching and learning of English, and the business of ELT is conducted.' E-mail is a convenient medium which gives students the experience of authentic writing tasks, in relation to fellow-students, teachers, and native-speaker contacts. It is now widely incorporated into language teaching – in those parts of the world where Internet access is routine – for a wide range of purposes, such as 'domestic' exchanges on everyday topics, teacher feedback on points of usage, exercises in business correspondence, and collaborative research projects. It is even possible to have the words of a text given an automatic grammatical parsing, using an e-mail connection. Additional textual and graphic material can be sent through the use of attachments. There have been several procedures devised for specific teaching purposes, such as the 'language learning in tandem' approach developed by David Little and others, in which people with different languages work together in pairs. Each participant sends messages in the other person's language, and provides feedback on problems of usage as they occur. The procedure also gives the participants the chance to learn about each other's character and culture, and exchange knowledge about their professional lives. The use of e-mail in this way certainly puts traditional methods of contact in the shade. I recall in 1960, after a multinational work experience in Europe, attempting to work in tandem with an Algerian Arab friend – my English in exchange for his Arabic. It lasted only a few weeks, simply because of the impracticability of the only method then available to us – exchange by slow and expensive letter. If e-mail had existed then, I would be a fluent Arabic speaker now, instead of being able to do little more than get through the first verse of 'Moustapha'.

The use of the Internet in foreign language teaching may be in its infancy, but it is plainly here to stay. Yet it already presents teachers with fresh challenges. The difficulties I noted earlier, arising out of the nature of the medium in conversation, apply with greater force to foreign learners – the lack of intonational cues, facial expressions, and so on. Also, teachers have to work out ways of handling a new kind of difficulty – new, at least, in the order of magnitude that it presents – namely, the fact that so much of the native-speaker usage in chatgroups and virtual worlds is non-standard, often ludic and highly deviant. The tolerance of typographical error, and the relaxation of the rules of spelling, punctuation and capitalization, will not in themselves be novelties to learners, for the same flexibility doubtless exists in their own mother-tongue Internet use. But foreign learners lack the intuitive sense of the boundary between standard and non-standard, or a sense of just how deviant a chatgroup usage might be, and by dint of exposure to repeated instances they may well end up misusing a construction, idiom, or other form. The bending and breaking of rules, which is a hallmark of ludic linguistic behaviour, always presents a problem to those who have not yet developed a confident command of the rules *per se*. Ironically, learners can sometimes give the impression that they are more fluent than they actually are, in that their errors can superficially resemble the deviant forms flamboyantly manifested by mother-tongue Internet users.

I have illustrated from technologies that are currently available. Already they are sufficient to introduce a huge range of new varieties to the English language (as to other languages), and their combined impact has brought us face-to-face with a new linguistic medium. But the story of twenty-first century English is only beginning. Computational futurologists are anticipating radical innovation in each of the three traditional domains of communication: production, transmission and reception. There will be extraordinary changes in delivery systems and access devices, and inconceivable increases in processing power. All of these will have an impact on the kind of language we use. The heart of the matter seems to be the immense increase in bandwidth, already seen in ISDN, cable, and optical fibre technologies, which will permit many channels to be simultaneously available within a single signal, and thus allow hitherto separate communication modalities to be integrated. The two main modes, sound and vision, have already begun to be linked in this way; and there is in principle no reason why other modes (tactile, olfactory, gustatory) should not also be incorporated. The various established media elements are already becoming increasingly integrated, in a frame of reference neatly captured by the phrase *streaming media*. It would appear that the aim is to make anything speedily available with anything – Web with sound and video, personal digital assistants with Web access, television with Internet access, Internet with television access, radio programmes with pictures, and so on. New terms are already evolving to describe the novel combinations of function, such as *teleputer*. Some domains, such as holography, have yet to develop their communicative nomenclature. It is difficult to resist the conclusion of one pair of commentators, Bob Cotton and Malcolm Garrett, who entitle their 1999 booklet on the future of the media and expert systems, *You ain't seen nothing yet*. That, of course, is what religious prophets used to say, too.

And for English language teachers, attempting to emulate prophets, the message is plain. Get familiar with the innovative language of the new technology as soon as you can; for the twenty-first century will see more linguistic change in English than we have seen at any time since the Renaissance. With language, too, we ain't seen nothing yet.

References

Crystal D (2001) *Language and the Internet*. Cambridge: Cambridge University Press.
The Jargon File at http://www.tuxedo.org/~est/jargon/
Wired Style: Principles of English Usage in the Digital Age (1999). New York: Broadway Books

10 CONFERENCE REVIEWS

10.1 Twenty-first century challenges

Patricia Lopez *The Anglo-Mexican Foundation, Mexico*

The 35th Annual Conference was once again held in Brighton, the city by the sea, famous for its picturesque Lanes. The Brighton Centre, opposite the seafront, was quite convenient for all the delegates who chose to stay in nearby hotels. Moreover, it offered the possibility of welcoming a large audience, who could attend most of the academic events within one self-contained building. In addition to the huge variety of talks and workshops, with something to suit everyone's needs and interests, the exhibition provided opportunities for delegates to find out about the latest products from various publishing houses, examination boards, schools, colleges and universities in the UK. Moreover, for the first time at an IATEFL Conference, there was an Internet Café (sponsored by Longman), where delegates could make use of a computer, though only for short periods, as it was a very popular spot!

The conference programme was quite impressive, with so many academic and social events that decisions were often difficult: throughout the four-day conference, there was an average of seventeen concurrent sessions running simultaneously within each slot.

It is always very enriching for somebody like me, who lives on the American Continent (northern hemisphere, to be more precise) to attend the IATEFL Conference. Even though our closest neighbours to the north of the Mexican Republic are the United States of America, and American influence is therefore ever-present, the organization I work for is a British-Mexican one. It was founded over half a century ago, with the purpose of bringing British and Mexican cultures closer together through language teaching. It is vital for us to be well-informed and aware of the current trends in ELT, as well as in education around the world, though it is of the utmost importance to know what is new in Britain, not only to confirm whether our organization is on the right track, but also to find ways in which innovation or change can be brought to bear, in teaching as well as in the design and development of new products. I have found that IATEFL is an ideal forum to keep up-to-date with worldwide developments in ELT. This is why I have chosen to concentrate on those issues which I believe represent the greatest challenges for ELT practitioners.

This year's conference will be remembered by many delegates as a landmark in the history of IATEFL, mainly due to the fact that for the first time, the opening plenary was delivered via a live video-conference link from the USA. Appropriately, Carol Chapelle's paper was about ELT, technology, and change. Carol's talk was full of stimulating ideas, informed by her own research, as regards the effects and implications of technology for EFL/ESL students. It was not surprising, though, to hear that despite the fact that people are interested in modern technology, not everybody feels at ease using it, and furthermore, it is difficult and expensive to keep up with it. Nevertheless, it was an exciting experience to witness what can be done with the help of modern technology (despite a few technical problems that had to be solved on the spot). Carol definitely gave the delegates a great deal of food for thought, and must have prompted many participants to start thinking of ways in which technology could be incorporated into their teaching practice. There were quite a few talks and workshops focusing on computers and the use of Internet for classroom activities. But it was striking to note that more than 90% of the sessions were still ignoring the potential of the new technologies. It appears that while the teaching profession is not rejecting these developments altogether, they are being cautious, and not taking the virtues of technology for granted. It seems to me that even if it is not yet practical for computer technology to be adopted in classrooms everywhere, it should certainly be considered as an important resource for both teachers and students.

One of the most outstanding features of the conference was undoubtedly the debate about the worldwide role of English staged by *The Guardian Weekly* and Macmillan Heinemann – *The Future of Global English*. All the contributions focused on the question of whether teachers should continue teaching 'native' English, or whether they should start teaching a lingua franca variety, which according to two of the speakers, would be a kind of hybrid European English. The key arguments supporting the latter view were as follows:

- the fact that for each native speaker of English in the world, there are four non-native English speakers
- languages are linked to the speakers' identities
- all languages should have the same rights
- English should not be privileged at the expense of minority languages
- while English should be used as a medium for international communication, non-native speakers should never lose their identities
- English as a lingua franca and English as a native language are two very different entities

The debate was well-organised and very professionally chaired by Will Hutton, the editor of *The Observer*, though it would have been interesting to learn how many of the delegates in the audience thought that the speakers' proposals were feasible. In addition, it would have been worth knowing what kind of language is going to be taught in Mexico, Central and South America, Asia and Africa. However, the question to reflect on is whether the world (and not only Europe) is willing and ready to embrace a 'stateless' language, very different from the native language that many of those present were taught, and have tried to teach to their students.

There were, as usual, the pre-conference events held by a number of the Special Interest Groups (SIGs), which I personally find very rewarding because for one day, delegates could concentrate on one single area of interest. All the SIGs were also allocated 'tracks' within the main conference, including the Open Forums which invited more active participation.

The conference closed with a final plenary session that was memorable for the wit and wisdom of the speaker, IATEFL's patron, Professor David Crystal. In his talk, entitled Twenty-first Century English, he spoke about the Internet and its impact on language, and speculated about how the language is likely to evolve during the twenty-first century.

I think that one of the many valuable things that delegates always take home with them from an IATEFL conference is the inspiration to reflect on their own teaching practice. However, on this occasion, they will also have to think about the challenges that ELT practitioners everywhere will have to face in the twenty-first century, and the question that Péter Medgyes challenged us to address: *Should we rejoice or apologise for the role we play in spreading English, often at the expense of other foreign languages?* It will be very interesting to see at the next IATEFL Annual Conference how some of the issues have evolved or changed in a year's time.

10.2 Reflections on the IATEFL conference

Kitty Loewenstein *Sprachinstitut der Industrie, Austria*

More than a month has passed since I returned from my first ever IATEFL conference in England, but it seems even longer. As Director of Studies of an extremely busy language school, I've been kept well occupied and hardly had a moment to myself. However, as I sit here trying to recall my experience of those four highly concentrated days in Brighton, I realise that two things have left a lasting impression – but more of that later.

Before setting off for Brighton I spoke to a few 'old hands' to make sure I really got the most out of the conference. Over the years I had heard the odd comments about there being too much choice and how easy it was to end up in the 'wrong' session and wish that you were sitting somewhere else. Here is a summary of their advice:

a) Don't spend too much time in workshops.
b) Spend your time networking, i.e. drink lots of coffee and don't go back in immediately when the breaks end.
c) Don't only go for the big names.
d) Go to the workshops of the lesser known.
e) Don't spend all your time with people you already know.
f) Take advantage of being in England and go shopping.

To give you an idea of how disobedient I am, what actually happened was:

- I went to a workshop/talk nearly every session, which meant I didn't stay put once the break was over (although I did drink plenty of tea, if not coffee).
- I went to see most of the big names.
- I went to only one workshop given by someone I had never heard of (and regretted it!)
- I spent most of my free time with old friends and enjoyed every minute of it.

The only piece of advice I *did* follow was to go shopping. However, when I returned to Vienna and got my MasterCard statement, I realised that had been a big mistake.

So, what did I get out of the many talks/workshops I so conscientiously attended? Two main things: First, my view of English as a lingua franca (i.e. living, developing, changing as opposed to Yorkshire vs Texan English) was one I was going to uphold and defend. Second, I was going to have to dedicate more time to e-learning in the future.

In my twenty years of teaching English and, in particular, my ten years of teaching Business English and ESP, I have become more and more certain of my aims. Essentially, I want to help my students express themselves in English in a manner that makes them feel comfortable. This means to say what they want, as they want and in the way they would naturally in their own language. In other words, to be themselves. Whether they can use the present perfect in the same way a native speaker might use it is immaterial if the above criteria have been satisfied. A highly competent German-speaking negotiator, presenter or secretary, for example, will want to give the same impression of his/her ability whether speaking in German or English. It is my job as an English teacher to ensure that s/he has the tools (the language and the confidence) to do this.

What I feel is so important for EFL teachers to realise is that English, as spoken by the native English speaker, need not or perhaps should not be our aim. It is neither feasible nor desirable. The reality is that there are two (if not many, many more) types of English – English as spoken by native speakers, and English as spoken by everybody else. However, it is the latter that is being spoken by people in business, science etc in meeting rooms all over the world, and who are we to tell them they should be speaking like us ('us' being, of course, native speakers of English). Judging by what I heard at the conference, this idea is beginning to take hold and I'm relieved to hear it.

While the talks on English as a lingua franca aroused me intellectually, the effect of the workshops on e-learning was completely different. These had implications of a much more practical nature. Since the conference, I have spent a great deal of time looking at recommended websites and the demos of the software that I found at the publishers' exhibition. There is no doubt that e-learning is an important product that language schools have to take seriously. I personally, however, did not hear or see anything at the conference that convinced me it is anything more than a useful support for teachers and learners. As for the quality of the material, I reserve judgement for the moment. Hopefully, by my next IATEFL conference, I will have something more positive to say. I sincerely hope so. As much as I hope that it does not take me so long to find the time for my next IATEFL conference as it did for the first one, because it was an extremely satisfying and enjoyable four days.

10.3 If your mobile phone rings, sing a song

Elena Angelova *Freelance, Bulgaria*

Some of the people who attended the 35th annual IATEFL conference in Brighton probably associate it with a number of sounds. The sounds at the Brighton Conference Centre ranged from songs to the ringing tones of mobile phones. Some members of the ELT community came to the decision that if a mobile phone rang in public, the owner would have to sing a song – also in public. Small wonder, then, that mobiles were mostly kept switched off during sessions, and I did not hear anybody singing a song at the presentations I went to. However, the conference venue was kept alive by stimulating talks and hearty laughter, announcements of prize-winners at the presentations and in the breaks. While listening to the presentations at the ELT Management SIG Open forum, we were able to tap our feet to *Yesterday* and a wonderful medley of golden oldies.

The Brighton conference was a landmark in my personal and professional life for several reasons. First, Brighton as a host city offers an incredibly wide range of opportunities for leisure, recreation and work. The atmosphere in the city is full of enjoyment and optimism, and a flowerpot perched precariously on top of some scaffolding was just one of the things which caught my attention. The opening night of the movie *Bridget Jones' Diary* was another incidental pleasure. The Brighton Conference Centre successfully accommodated more than 1500 participants from over 70 countries. The weather was good (most of the time), and there were all the prerequisites for a rewarding conference.

In my opinion, some 'firsts' set this conference apart from previous ones. For the first time ever, the conference included an opening plenary given via a live transatlantic video-conference link. The plenary (given by Carol Chapelle, Professor of Applied Linguistics at Iowa State University, USA) was sponsored by the TOEFL program at Educational Testing Service (ETS) and, although it did not go without a hitch, the idea of this kind of delivery is very exciting.

Another innovation I must mention is the Internet café sponsored by Longman. The café was widely used by the delegates and contributed a great deal to the convenience of conference participants. The access to inboxes and the Net made this area in the exhibition hall quite a magnet.

A very positive feature of the Brighton conference was the way in which newcomers were catered for. A series of meetings was arranged to help first–time attenders get the most out of what is undoubtedly the largest ELT forum in Europe. The conference programme included a very useful page of tips for newcomers. I would like to paraphrase a popular proverb: a conference is in the eye of the beholder. The benefits we may get from a conference are very much up to us. However, first-time attenders and first-time presenters would have benefited from a short induction highlighting the existence of up to twenty parallel sessions, to say nothing of publisher-sponsored presentations with promotional freebies. For me, this aspect of advertising and public relations was a very positive extra!

Discussions enjoyed over the breakfast table in our small hotel added to the whole experience. These cosy chats and the exchange of impressions confirmed the opinion expressed by one delegate that some of the most important and interesting things were happening in the breaks and during informal discussions. In addition to these early-morning chats, there was the opportunity to sign up for informal lunchtime discussion sessions with the plenary speakers.

The Brighton conference was a future-oriented professional convention with the innovations introduced and the new opportunities available to delegates. A few presentations acquainted the audience with the basic requirements to get one's material published. Some presenters told us of their involvement in various projects and were on the lookout for future collaboration. Some of the first offers of cooperation started filling our inboxes while we were still at the conference. The availability of delegates' e-mail addresses in the conference programme also made it possible for publishers to approach us directly.

The academic level of the presentations, workshops, discussions was as intellectually challenging as usual. The wide variety of ELT issues addressed by the speakers included in the programme must have satisfied even the most demanding tastes. I personally found the sessions on global issues affecting the profession extremely thought-provoking.

Presentations focusing on the role of ELT practitioners as part of the community and the importance of the social context of teaching raised some of the most relevant issues. And when presented with humour, which did not lessen the importance of the issues, the laughter was accompanied by a huge dose of reflection for homework.

On the whole, I think that Brighton 2001 will have contributed substantially to the record of IATEFL annual conferences not just by being informative, but by offering choices. I see this conference as a wide window open to the future. How wide we decide to open it depends entirely on us.

Editor's note: Bibliographies and references are given in full for Plenary papers, but are not included with reports. Readers wishing to follow up bibliographical references can obtain the relevant details on application to the authors, or to the editor in cases where no contact information is given.